GAMES
(& OTHER STUFF)
FOR TEACHERS

CLASSROOM ACTIVITIES
THAT PROMOTE
PRO-SOCIAL LEARNING

CHRIS CAVERT, LAURIE FRANK & FRIENDS

Published by:

Wood 'N' Barnes Publishing & Distribution
2717 NW 50th
Oklahoma City, OK 73112
(405) 942-6812

Photographs by Chris Cavert, Susana Acosta & Lauren Baikie
Illustrations by Chris Cavert, Susana Acosta & Todd Staggs
Cover Art by Blu Designs.
Copyediting & Design by Ramona Cunningham.

Printed in the United States of America
Oklahoma City, Oklahoma
ISBN # 1-885473-22-2

To order copies of this book, please call:
Jean Barnes Books
405-946-0621 • 800-678-0621

PLAY FOR PEACE

All royalties from this publication will be donated to **PLAY FOR PEACE.**

PURPOSE

Play for Peace brings children of conflicting cultures together through cooperative play to promote positive relationships among people who have a history of inter-cultural tension. By bringing children with unique backgrounds, values and beliefs together through the seemingly simple act of play, seeds of compassion are sown for a more peaceful today and tomorrow.

OBJECTIVES

- To promote positive relationships among children from cultures in conflict.
- To create a non-threatening environment, free from fear, where children can experience the joy of play.
- To influence the behavior of adults through the positive example of children at play.
- To draw positive global attention to areas in the world which experience negative media exposure.

VISION

Play for Peace is a process of community building. Rather than being an event or program, it is the creation of ongoing learning partnerships that free each child to build positive life-long connections with others. Especially among people with a history of inter-cultural tension, cooperative play is one of the few bridges that promotes positive cross-cultural relationships.

It is the intent of Play for Peace that children throughout the world will someday have the opportunity to experience the ways in which we are all connected, develop compassion for others, and share laughter with people that are "different" from themselves.

Play for Peace has already been active in Chicago; the Middle East; the Balkans; in Central America; in South Africa; and is expanding into other parts of the world. For more information on how you can support Play for Peace, write:

Play for Peace
P.O. Box 6205
Buffalo Grove, IL 60089 U.S.A.
(847) 520-1444
info@playforpeace.org

— OUR DEDICATION —

This book is dedicated to all students and their teachers.
May you always have fun together.

— OUR THANKS —

This project would not have been possible without the myriad of people who
contributed their time, ideas, spirit, and most of all their love
to see this through. If we forget any of you in our thanks, we apologize.
Please know we appreciate you.

First, to all the activity contributors. In some way your ideas made it to these pages.
(We'll do it like the movies - in order of appearance.)
Jim Cain, Karl Rohnke, Larry Eckert, Highlights for Children, Frank Aycox,
Frank Harris, John Newstrom, Edward Scannell & McGraw Hill, Craig Dobkin,
Clifford Knapp, Jackie Gerstein, Scott Trent, Kathy Hellenbrand, Sam Sikes,
Joel Cryer, Donna Allen, Kenny Allen, Kip Prichard, and Jack Canfield.
From the way down deep bottom of our hearts, thank you.
Together we will touch many lives.

Next we would like to thank Good Shepherd Episcopal School in Dallas, Texas,
and Jeanne Harvey's Shepherds Pi staff and kids.
Especially Jeanne herself for helping us get the pictures we needed.
Also, to Lauren Baikie, Lauren Bittner, Rachel Cone, James Farris, Ty Martin,
Kelsey Martin, Anita Pandian, Stephanie Parker, Katherine Shuey,
Hunter Veirs, and Kristen Williams.
You are all great!!
Thanks so much for your extra time and expert modeling.

Thanks to our colleagues Mitch Clark, Kathy McCausland,
Betsy Pool, and Honorary Professor Jaime Domingues.
We appreciate all that you do for the children in your lives.

A very extra special thanks goes to Susana Acosta
for all the time she contributed to this project.
You are a gift to us all.

Thanks goes out to Sharen for the picture coupons.

To Mony Cunningham. We thank you for your insight, creativity, patience,
and most of all your fun spirit. You have outdone yourself again.

Finally to our foremost teachers, our parents.
Thank you for being there for us.

TOGETHER WE MAKE A DIFFERENCE!

INTRODUCTION —

You have in your hands GAMES (& OTHER STUFF) FOR TEACHERS –a special project put together by teachers for teachers. The activities in this book focus on developing pro-social skills that will help both children and adults interact in a positive and caring way. The activities are meant to be fun and easy to read. All necessary equipment can be obtained within the classroom or school setting. Sample questions are provided with each activity for discussion purposes, and variations are also provided to help you adjust to the skill levels of your students.

GAMES (& OTHER STUFF) FOR TEACHERS contains sit-down, get up & go, as well as paper and pencil activities appropriate for students ages eight and older. With very little extra planning you will be able to implement the individual and group efforts that focus on a wide variety of pro-social skills such as listening, following directions, cooperation, diversity, patience, persistence, and many others. If these skills can be learned in the classroom, there is a chance they may be used outside of the classroom to enhance the interaction of students' lives and communities.

GAMES (& OTHER STUFF) FOR TEACHERS is an experiential activity book. If you haven't done so already, we recommend that you explore other resources within the field of experiential education to better understand the implementation of these types of activities (see Resources sections). Most, if not all, of the activities in this book are straight forward and are easy to present. However, to get the most out of your time and each activity, you might want to learn more about the intended process.

BEFORE YOU DIVE IN:

The one part of experiential methodology we do not want to leave out is Challenge by Choice, developed by Project Adventure, a leading organization in the field of experiential education. "The concept of Challenge by Choice allows each person to be in control of his/her level of participation. It means that a person may choose what s/he wishes to share with the group about him/herself. It means that a person may choose to be totally involved physically and emotionally in an activity, or choose to sit back and watch. It does not mean that a person sits and reads the newspaper while the group goes about its business. No matter what level of participation an individual chooses, s/he is still part of the group, even if it means being an observer" (Frank, 2000). We would hope that you make every effort to use Challenge by Choice in your classrooms. It is a proven way to build trust within your classroom community and promotes the spirit of experiential education.

USING GAMES (& OTHER STUFF) FOR TEACHERS:

Each activity is broken down into some specifics: Possible Objectives, Needs, Procedure, Observations/Questions, Variations, and Other Ideas.

POSSIBLE OBJECTIVES: As teachers we are often called upon to write lesson plans that contain objectives. We have provided some social skill objectives for you here. For every activity in this book there are some common social skills: Risk Taking, Following Directions, Willingness, Participation, and Fun. So, always remember to add these to your list.

NEEDS: This section describes the equipment and supplies you will need for each activity. Most you will be able to find in your classroom. A few things, like balloons, you might have to bring in. Most activities will need little preparation. A few will need a little extra time.

PROCEDURE: This section describes one (or maybe two) possible ways to implement the activity within your classroom. If you are a kinesthetic learner, some of the descriptions might be difficult to figure out. In this case, do the best that you can. Once you put some action to the words, you will see what works and what doesn't work. Please, don't hesitate to make the changes you need to better fit your classroom. Whatever you do - HAVE FUN WITH IT!

OBSERVATIONS/QUESTIONS: Here we have provided some ideas for you to work with, before, during, or after the activity. These questions can help you understand a little bit more about what the activity might bring out in the group. There is also some space provided to write some of your own questions. Using these questions with the activities turns a recreational endeavor into an experiential process, which we want to encourage in the use of this book. This part of experiential education is not easy to implement. As we suggested above, please take some additional time to explore the resources available on processing to better understand how to use it.

VARIATIONS: Almost all of the activities in this book have at least one variation. Use these variations to change the challenge level to fit your class. They can also be used to progress more slowly into activities so your class can build on successes. Feel free to adapt any of these ideas (or any activity for that matter) to fit your situation.

OTHER IDEAS: Here is some open space to write your variations and ideas on the activity.

OTHER HELPFUL STUFF:

We have provided a wide variety of resources for you to explore. We know how limited your time as a teacher is, so we just ask that you do the best that you can to find out more about the processes of experiential education.

See Appendix A for the Community Building Sequence Chart that links the activities in GAMES (& OTHER STUFF) FOR TEACHERS with Laurie's book, "A Journey Into the Land of Heart: Creating Community in the Classroom and Beyond" (due to be published in early 2000). Laurie's book will provide an outstanding introduction into the process of experiential education and help you develop strong community building within a classroom setting. Cooperation, trust and problem-solving are part of the Community Building Sequence described in her book. You will be able to use the activities in GAMES (& OTHER STUFF) FOR TEACHERS to coincide with this sequence.

Also, don't forget about the possibility of hosting a workshop (see pg. 158). We would be more than happy to visit and play with you.

We hope you will enjoy using this book.

Chris & Laurie

CONTENT

Acknowledgements   iv
Introduction   v

Are You More Like...   1
Now & Later   4
Quality Assurance   6
The Big Question/30 Seconds   10
You Tear Me Up   16
Classroom Assumptions   18
Chosen   23
Letter Opener   25
Assumption Test   27
Number Game   29
Group Number Game   34
P.S.   37
Simply Paper   39
Empathy   42
Blue Cards   47
Pencil, Paper, Popsicle Stick   49
Particulars   51
Roomination   55
Enumeration   59
Classroom Poetry   63
It's All in the Cards   73
Circle-a-Loons   83
Balloon Bash   85
Objectables   88
Over the Top   90
A What?   93
Quick Numbers   95
Touch   97
Sensory Masterpiece   99
The Mixing Game   105
Front-to-Front   107

CONTENT (con't.)

Cliques   109
Community Box   112
Gotcha Lines   114
Centerpiece   117
A Very Large Knot   119
Toe Jam   121
Classroom Parts   123
Don't Spill the Beans   125
Chris-Cross   127
Poker Face   130
Peer Pressure   132
Wired   135
Driving in the Dark   137
Book Return   140
Challenge Field   143
Experiential Lunch   145
The Shoes   148
The Car Wash   150

Community Building Sequence   151
References/Resources   155
Additional Experiential References   156
About the Authors   157
Workshop Information   158

ARE YOU MORE LIKE...? —

POSSIBLE OBJECTIVES: Decision Making, Accepting Diversity, Listening, Compromising...

NEEDS: You will need a line on the floor for this one - circular or straight. You could use masking tape or an activity rope of some sort if you have one.

PROCEDURE: Clear the center of the room as much as possible (you will find as you read on that I like to "clear the center of the room" a lot - gets the oxygen moving). If the straight line is easiest for you, just place some masking tape down the center of the floor. I'll use the circle formation here in my description.

Ask your students to stand around the outside of the circle. You will ask them to decide on one of two choices from each question you are going to ask. If they are more like the first choice, step into the circle. If they are more like the second choice, stay to the outside of the circle. Leave a little time between each question to give the students a chance to see who is standing with them. I will play this one too, just stepping in and out as I read.

That's the simple gist. I like to use this activity as my introduction to the process of active learning - getting up and moving around. I keep it simple the first time with just a little processing after. Down the road I can use this activity again to bring out more personal perspectives on the questions.

> **NOTE:** I have had a great deal of fun with this activity. I try to encourage my students to think more about the characteristics of the choices. I will often hear, "But I don't like either." You might help them a bit by describing some of the characteristics of the items. This might help them "get out of the box" so to speak.

The list below is not in any sort of order. You can pick and choose the questions that will serve your purpose at the time. You might want to add questions of your own.

ARE YOU MORE LIKE...
chocolate or strawberries?
a carpet or a wood floor?
a hard cover or paperback book?
skim milk or 2%?
a chair or a couch?
apples or oranges?
pants or shorts?
a bath or a shower?
jeans or khakis?
glass or plastic?

a bunk bed or a twin bed?
a bus or a plane?
a bracelet or a necklace?
solids or stripes?
sandals or shoes?
shade or sun?
cursive or printing?
buttered or plain popcorn?
potato chips or pretzels?
a run or a walk?
soda or water?
panic or relaxed?
gel or paste?
a weekday or a weekend?
Chic Filet® or McDonalds®?
long hair or short hair?
fact or fiction?
Air mail or E-mail?
peanut or plain?
a cat or a dog?
salted or unsalted?
the escalator or the stairs?
a chocolate or oatmeal cookie?
Cheerios® or corn flakes?
math or art?
country or rock music?
the ocean or a river?
a pen or a pencil?
fish or steak?
a desk top or lap top computer?
7UP® or Sprite®?
diet or regular?
pasta or rice?
cheese or pepperoni?
hamburgers or hot dogs?
an amusement park or a water park?
Army or Navy?
fruit or vegetable?
television or radio?
a CD or a cassette?

OBSERVATIONS/QUESTIONS:

·Who can think of another pair to choose from?
·Did anyone have trouble deciding? Why?
·How many of you might have made a choice based on what one of your friends decided?
·Did anyone not want to step into the center even if you were more like the first choice? Why?
·Was there ever just one person in the center?..on the outside? What was that like?
·Is it hard to make choices sometimes? What makes it difficult?
·What sorts of choices might we be making in our classroom?
·Will we all make the same choices? Why not?
·What might be some negative aspects of being different?
·What are some skills we might need to practice to work through our differences in this class?
·What might be some positive aspects of being willing to be different?
·
·

(OTHERS)

VARIATIONS:

·If you want to add a choice for undecideds or the "would rather hear finger nails dragged across the chalkboard than pick one of the two," then have these students put one foot into the circle and leave one foot outside the circle. Do the same students "sit on the fence"? Why?

OTHER IDEAS:

3

NOW & LATER—

POSSIBLE OBJECTIVES: Sharing, Listening, Accepting Diversity, Verbal Communication, Helping, Attention to Task...

NEEDS: Each student will need a plain paper folder. I like to find the ones that have the three hole tabs in them so I can attach papers as well as put papers in the pockets. You will also need a lot of old magazines to cut up, some scissors, and some non-toxic rubber cement.

PROCEDURE: In most cases the students can find and buy their own folders. Provide an example for them to see so they know what to get. Nothing fancy because they will be gluing pictures on it. You can also ask each student to bring in a few old magazines from home. Be sure they understand that the magazines will be cut up.

This activity involves a few stages over a period of time. The practical use of the folder is for storing all the paper activities that we might be doing from this book - as well as other memorable items. The symbolic use of the folder will be to show others a little bit about who we are, what we might consider doing in the future, as well as how we feel about things in general.

I usually work on the front cover of the folder first. This will be the "now" side. Cut out pictures, words and/or letters to make words that represent the individual at the present time. Things we like to do, places we like to go, food we like to eat. We might work on this over a period of a week. When everyone finishes, take the opportunity to sit together in a large circle and share the "now." Always remember that every student has the right to share as well as not share.

Whenever the folders are not in use I collect and store them in a safe place for the next time we need them. It has been my experience that if the folders leave the room, they might not make it back.

After a few weeks of getting to know each other, work on the back part of the folder. This is the "later" portion. Find pictures and such that represent some things we are considering for the future, e.g., what sort of cars we might drive, what occupations we might be interested in, where we might live, where we might travel, and so on. When everyone is finished, share the "later."

When you think your group is ready to share more personal aspects of their life, then work on the inside of the folder. The front of the pockets is a good place for feeling words, names of family and friends, special places, special pets. I like to bring in a picture of my family members and glue it on the inside so I can share it with the kids. The discussion over the inside tends to be on more of a personal level. To do this, students should have a good level of trust with each other so they can feel free to share the more personal aspects of their lives. This trust is built, we hope, over the year through activities and experiences they have shared together. Use your best judgement on when to present this step.

Process each step of this activity as you see fit. Since many of the students will be sharing their folder, you might not be able to fit in any other processing.

OBSERVATIONS/QUESTIONS:

- Who is working on their folder?
- Who is having a hard time working on their folder?
- Who "can't" find any pictures? Why?
- Who is helping others find pictures? Who's helping others more than themselves?
- Whose folder is filled up? Whose is not?
- What are the future goals of your students? Are their goals positive or negative? Are there any students who have no perspective of their future?
- What is your favorite picture on your folder? Why?

(OTHERS)
-
-

VARIATIONS:

- There is a great activity I learned from Jack Canfield at one of his seminars. It's called "What's on my mind?" Pair up students. Have them draw single-lined silhouettes of each other on a large sheet of paper. After they are finished, have them find pictures/words in magazines that represent the things on their minds and glue them on their silhouettes. Put these pictures up around the room and discuss them from time to time.

OTHER IDEAS:

QUALITY ASSURANCE—

POSSIBLE OBJECTIVES: Sharing, Verbal Communication, Persistence, Decision Making, Helping...

NEEDS: Each student will need a pencil and a "Quality Assurance Worksheet."

PROCEDURE: When each student has the needed supplies, ask them to look over the qualities on the sheet. Based on the qualities listed, have them fill in the two blank squares with a couple of qualities that they want to find in the class. When everyone has filled in the empty squares, ask them to mingle around the room. During said mingling, have the students get as many signatures on their Quality Assurance Worksheets as they can before you say stop. Students signing a quality square must be related to the quality or characteristic in the square. Students may not sign any sheet more than once. They may sign their own sheet - but only once.

I usually don't set a time limit for this activity up front. I like to monitor the level of participation and call a stop to it when the energy is going down. If someone completes their entire sheet before the time is up, just keep an eye on them to see what happens. If they ask you what they should do when they are finished (and most do), just tell them to stay in the room until the activity is over - leave the door open (figuratively speaking - because they are staying in the room) for some choice here. "To be or not to be helpful" is the question.

I like to play this activity (meaning I play too) with my students during the "getting to know each other" stage near the beginning of the year. It's a good way to discover some new things about each other.

OBSERVATIONS/QUESTIONS:
- Who was really working to get signatures? What seemed to be their motivation?
- What did you like about this activity?
- What was the most difficult part of the activity?
- Would anyone like to share some of the traits they wrote in the empty boxes?
- Why did you write these traits down? Do you have these two traits?
- What did you do when you were finished? Help anyone? Why? Why not?
- Did anyone find out something new about any of their classmates?
- How many of the qualities on the sheet do you match up with?
- What would be important about learning some of the qualities of our classmates?
- Did you learn anything about your teacher?
- What sorts of qualities do you think make up a good teacher?
- What sorts of qualities make up a good student?
- What sorts of qualities make up a good classroom community?
-
-

(OTHERS)

VARIATIONS:

·Play like Bingo®. See if everyone can achieve five in a row before the time is up.
·Make up your own sheet (we provided a blank one for you) with qualities that fit your particular group. This is a good way for the students to discover some special abilities and successes of others. Making up your own sheet allows you to change qualities as the year goes along. You start out very general and get more specific as the group matures.

OTHER IDEAS:

QUALITY ASSURANCE WORKSHEET

has blue eyes?	likes math?	rides a bike to school?	doesn't have pierced ears?	is the oldest child in your family?
likes drawing?	carries a blue backpack?	has a website?	is on a basket-ball team?	likes pizza?
plays a musical instrument?	likes to read?	wears size 10 shoes?	likes to cook?	doesn't have a driver's license?
likes activities like this?	favorite sub-ject is PE?	likes winter?	has two sisters?	likes scary movies?
wants to become a teacher?	likes spinach?	wants to be a foreign-exchange student?	likes to sit in the back?	has naturally curly hair?
is a good listener?	has a birthday in October?	likes classical music?		

Are you a person who:

QUALITY ASSURANCE WORKSHEET

30 SECONDS & THE BIG QUESTION—
Jim Cain

POSSIBLE OBJECTIVES: Verbal Communication, Sharing, Decision Making, Listening...

NEEDS: Each student will need a 3" x 5" blank note card and a pencil. If you plan to use the questions included with this activity, then make a copy for yourself. This way you can check off the questions you ask and return to the unasked portion at another time.

PROCEDURE: Clear a big open space in your room.

30 SECONDS

Partner up - a group of three will work fine also if you need to make one. (You could play as well, just carry the questions around with you.) Ask the students to formally introduce themselves to their partner. Now, ask the students a question from the question sheets (see pgs. 12-15). The pairs have 30 seconds total to share their answers with each other. If you want to give them a 15 second warning as a switch cue you can. After 30 seconds, call "change." Each student has to find a different partner to stand with. Repeat the process: formal introduction, question, 30 seconds. "Change." Continue the process as long as the energy is good.

30 SECONDS provides an opportunity for interaction with many students in the class. The children can learn a bit more about each other and practice those communication skills.

THE BIG QUESTION

Either of these two games can be played separately, but I like to use them one after the other. During 30 SECONDS the students are asked questions. Using these questions as a model the students tend to present more interesting questions for THE BIG QUESTION. If THE BIG QUESTION is played by itself, some groups struggle to come up with questions because they are not really sure what sort of things they could ask. Anyway, on with the game.

Give each student a blank 3" x 5" note card. Ask each student to write on the card a question they might ask:

(choose any one of these ideas or make up another)

-someone when they first meet.
-their favorite actress or actor.
-someone in their classroom.
-a friend.
-their parents.
-the President.

10

When everyone has a question, pair up. Have them politely introduce themselves. Give the pairs 30 seconds to ask and answer their two questions. After 30 seconds ask the students to exchange cards with their present partner, then find a different partner. Repeat the process: introduction, 30 seconds for questions, exchange cards, change partners. Continue the game as long as the energy is good.

If I have the time I like to collect all the cards. At random, I'll pick a card and ask the question to the entire class to find out some of the answers that were given and maybe even come up with a few more.

Mr. Cain shared one of the most interesting ponderables so far: "Where does the white go after the snow melts?"

OBSERVATIONS/QUESTIONS:
·Was the activity easy or hard for you? Explain?
·Was 30 seconds too long or too short?
·Did you learn anything new about your classmates? Did any of their responses surprise you? Why?
·Who remembers their original question? Did you get a satisfactory answer?
·Did you learn anything new from the questions that were traded to you?
·What is the importance of asking questions?
·Is it hard or difficult for you to ask questions?
·What prevents you from asking questions?
·How can we encourage each other to ask questions in this class?
(OTHERS) ·
·

VARIATIONS:
·As you play 30 SECONDS pass the sheet of questions to different students. When the question asker says "change," she passes the paper to someone else.
·For THE BIG QUESTION, have the students write questions on a class review topic so they can study while they play.

OTHER IDEAS:
·For 1,001 questions to help open your students' minds and generate creative thinking and problem-solving, buy a copy of Larry Eckert's "If Anybody Asks Me..." (see References).

"30 SECONDS" QUESTIONS

1. If it weren't for school, what do you think you would you be doing? Why?
2. Describe how you know you are in a good school.
3. What is the most valuable way you can help your school? Why?
4. In what way do you hope this will be a better year? How can you help make it happen?
5. How would it be to have year-round school? Why?
6. How much authority should students have in setting school policies? Why?
7. Your school has a suggestion box. What idea(s) would you write to make your school a better place? Why?
8. How would you feel about being MC of a program in front of all the students and teachers? Why?
9. What's your opinion about male cheerleaders in high school? Why, or why not?
10. What school subject would you rather study without a textbook? Why?
11. All the students stand, clap and cheer one day when you enter the room. How would you feel? Why?
12. Who gets more respect at your school - females or males? How can you tell?
13. Should high school students be required to do community service before they graduate? Why, or why not?
14. Should PE be a requirement in school? Why, or why not?
15. When is it appropriate to share your homework? Why?
16. Some public schools run male-only and female-only classes. If you had the chance, would you go to a school like this? Why, or why not?
17. How do students at your school treat other students who are 'different'? Do you approve of this treatment? Why, or why not?
18. Do you see high school graduation more as the 'end' or the 'beginning' for you? In what way?
19. A student can legally drop out of high school any time after 16 years of age. Is this law reasonable, or should every student be required to complete 12 grades? Why?
20. If you were on your school's Student Council, how motivational do you think you could be to the rest of the students? Why?
21. Would you rather attend a large school with hundreds of students, or a smaller school of about two hundred? Why?
22. The Board of Education in your town asks your opinion about making the school day longer for all students. What would you tell them? Why?

GAMES (& other stuff) FOR TEACHERS, © 1999 CHRIS CAVERT/WOOD 'N' BARNES PUBLISHING & DISTRIBUTION
QUESTIONS, "IF ANYBODY ASKS ME..." by LARRY ECKERT, © 1998 WOOD 'N' BARNES PUBLISHING & DISTRIBUTION

"30 SECONDS" QUESTIONS

23. When your teacher and parents disagree on something, who do you usually tend to side with? Why?

24. Other than actually being ill, what would be a reason important enough for you to call in 'sick' to school? Has this ever happened?

25. Considering your worst memory of school so far, how well could you live through that if it happened again? Why?

26. Should school officials be able to check out student lockers? Why, or why not? If so, under what conditions?

27. Should a very above-average student be allowed to move ahead a grade or two? Why, or why not?

28. You are an exceptionally gifted student. Assuming it was your own choice, would you want to move ahead a grade or two? Why, or why not?

29. Your school asks for suggestions on how to make the library more valuable to students. What suggestion would you give? Why?

30. Most students do not like school-prepared lunches. What ideas would you have for making lunches more popular, affordable, and at the same time, still as nutritious as possible?

31. What is the most effective technique you use in studying for a test?

32. How much of a friend do you think teachers should be with their students? Why?

33. Do teachers in your school handle discipline problems well, or could it be done more effectively? How?

34. If you were a teacher, how would you keep students your age interested in learning?

35. As a school principal, you become aware that several students are getting permanent tattoos, resulting in a great deal of extra attention from their peers. What would your reaction be? Why?

36. What is the worst test you have ever had in school? What made it that way?

37. What type of student in your school seems to get the most respect from peers? How can you tell?

38. If your school could win the state championship in one sport, which sport would you want it to be? Why?

39. Should there be any consequences for a student found smoking at school? Why, or why not?

40. Many schools have a "no hat" policy in their buildings. Is this a good policy, or not? Why?

GAMES (& other stuff) FOR TEACHERS, © 1999 CHRIS CAVERT/WOOD 'N' BARNES PUBLISHING & DISTRIBUTION
QUESTIONS, "IF ANYBODY ASKS ME..." by LARRY ECKERT, © 1998 WOOD 'N' BARNES PUBLISHING & DISTRIBUTION

"30 SECONDS" QUESTIONS

41. At school, what is the most comfortable room for you to be in? Why?

42. While you are at school, what is your greatest worry or concern? Why?

43. You hear that your school staff is considering requiring all students to wear uniforms. They say it will help build unity and cut down on discipline problems. What would you say? Why?

44. What are some good things about going to a new school?

45. What style of clothing would not be "cool" at your school? Why not?

46. Which school subject seems the most pointless to you? In what ways?

47. Which school subject seems the most valuable to you? In what ways?

48. If you could make one change in your school's dress code, what would that change be? Why?

49. If you wrote the school policy, would there be any consequences for students not attending classes? If so, what would you recommend? Why?

50. Your principal wants your input on the school's attendance policy. How would you make it fair and appropriate for all students?

51. Should students be allowed to retake a test as many times as necessary in order to finally pass it? Why, or why not?

52. How many people know your locker combination? How safe do you feel with that?

53. Does a teacher have any responsibility to students who fail their test? If so, what are those responsibilities?

54. How much homework is too much? How can you tell?

55. A new school will be grouping their students for classes by ability level in each subject rather than by age. If you had a choice, would you go to this school? Why, or why not?

56. What can someone in your school do to become popular? Why is that effective?

57. Are there any advantages for students who go to an all-boys' or an all-girls' school? Why, or why not? If so, what are some?

58. What new student activities could your school include to make it a more interesting place? Why?

59. In your school, are girls given the opportunity to be seen as equally smart as boys? Why, or why not?

60. A girl at your school wants to go out for wrestling. How do you think most other students will react to the news? Why?

61. In your school, is it important for students to be aware of cultural and ethnic differences? Why, or why not?

GAMES (& other stuff) FOR TEACHERS, © 1999 CHRIS CAVERT/WOOD 'N' BARNES PUBLISHING & DISTRIBUTION
QUESTIONS, "IF ANYBODY ASKS ME..." by LARRY ECKERT, © 1998 WOOD 'N' BARNES PUBLISHING & DISTRIBUTION

"30 SECONDS" QUESTIONS

62. Should high schools require a class on effective parenting techniques before graduation? Why, or why not?

63. Large class size is a problem in many schools. What would you say is the perfect number of students for a class? Why?

64. What would you do if you got to school and realized that the very important take-home math test was left at home? Why?

65. Many people think history is an important subject to study. Would you agree? Why, or why not?

66. What is the best meal that your school serves? Which meal could definitely NOT be called their best? Why?

67. How do you know when you are sitting in the wrong place in the lunch room?

68. Do students in your classes treat each other with enough respect? How can you tell?

69. At the beginning of a new class, when you are allowed to sit in the desk of your choice, which desk are you most likely to take? Why?

70. At school, one group hangs together and tells each other all the secrets they have heard; another group gets together but, generally, keeps their secrets private and unmentioned. Which group would you feel most comfortable around? Why?

71. Suppose your school allowed you one day off to either follow a worker of your choice while they performed their job, or to visit a college campus of your choice. Which would you choose? Why? What would you hope to learn?

72. A new student, who cannot speak a word of English, joins your class. What would your behavior, or reaction be to this person? Why?

73. Is your school doing everything possible to prepare you for life after graduation? If not, what more would you suggest?

74. A certain movie would be perfect to explain the subject your class is studying in school; however, it has an 'R' rating. Should it be allowed in class? Why, or why not?

GAMES (& other stuff) FOR TEACHERS, © 1999 CHRIS CAVERT/WOOD 'N' BARNES PUBLISHING & DISTRIBUTION
QUESTIONS, "IF ANYBODY ASKS ME..." by LARRY ECKERT, © 1998 WOOD 'N' BARNES PUBLISHING & DISTRIBUTION

YOU TEAR ME UP—

Karl Rohnke

POSSIBLE OBJECTIVES: Accepting Diversity, Listening, Decision Making, Sharing...

NEEDS: You will need a blank piece of 8 1/2" x 11" paper for each student.

PROCEDURE: Hand each student a sheet of paper. Ask them to each do their own work - "Even though there are others around you, please do your own work." Tell the students that they are not allowed to ask or answer any questions during the activity, but they can talk freely among themselves. When everyone is ready, give the following directions, in order, repeating each direction twice and giving the next direction only when each student has completed the stated direction (don't move on until everyone is ready).

1. Fold the paper in half and tear off the bottom left hand corner. Save this corner.
2. Fold the paper in half again and tear off the upper right hand corner. Save this corner.
3. Fold the paper in half again and tear off the upper left hand corner. Save this corner.

When every student is finished, open up the papers and compare the results. Snowflakes. What do we know about snowflakes?

> NOTE: If a student does ask you what to do. Tell them they must decide for themselves.

OBSERVATIONS/QUESTIONS:

- Are any of the snowflakes the same? Why/why not?
- Did anyone ask questions during the activity? What were the directions?
- Was it frustrating not to be able to ask questions?
- Were you able to do your own work?
- Did anyone look at another person's work for ideas?
- What do you think about getting ideas from someone else? Copying?
- Has there ever been a time when you gave someone directions and they didn't do what you expected them to do?
- How can we eliminate some of the confusion about following directions?
- How many of you have a hard time asking questions? Why?

(OTHERS)
-
-

VARIATIONS:

· Feel free to make up your own directions. Keep in mind that if you fold an 8 1/2" x 11" sheet of paper more than three times it is very difficult to tear.

· Karl suggests to blindfold students or have them close their eyes during the activity. This works well if you don't want to open the doors that keeping your eyes open open. (I had to read that again, too!)

· Another option along the same line is to ask students to draw shapes on their paper following your instructions. For example: Draw a small circle. Draw a square so the bottom right hand corner touches the circle. Put a diamond in the square, and so on.

OTHER IDEAS:

· What if you had students ask questions and you answered them? What if you told them all "exactly" where to fold and tear? Would the papers be the same?

CLASSROOM ASSUMPTIONS —
Highlights® for Children

POSSIBLE OBJECTIVES: Accepting Diversity, Inclusion, Decision Making, Consensus...

NEEDS: Sitting at their desks, each student will need a copy of the "Classroom" handout, a blank sheet of paper and something to write with. It would also be ideal if you could make an overhead of this handout to aid in the discussion process - then, of course, you will need an overhead projector.

PROCEDURE: Ask your students to pretend it is their first day at a new school. Hand each student the picture of their new class, complete with new students. Ask the children in your class to write a word or two that they would use to describe each new classmate in the picture. (Depending on your time line, you could also just have them write on a few students of their choice.) Give the students enough time to fill in the sheet and then discuss their perceptions. Using the overhead can help to identify the person in question.

I have seen quite a bit of difference in the responses of my younger students as compared to my older ones. The discussions I have had with the younger children seem to focus more on assumptions, where the discussions with the older kids seem to turn more to reputations and the assumptions that stem from them. (The overhead variation has worked very well with my older students.)

For an added adventure, after the students have shared their perceptions, read the short histories of each student we have provided.

OBSERVATIONS/QUESTIONS:
- Was this activity easy or difficult? What made it that way?
- How many of you had the same idea about one of the students in the classroom handout? Who is correct?
- How can we find out if the assumptions are correct?
- What is an assumption? Are they good or bad?
- When can assumptions be bad? When can they be good?
- Would anyone be willing to share an assumption they have made that turned out to be untrue?
- How about an assumption that turned out to be true?
- What can we do in this classroom if we make or hear an assumption about someone?
- How could this help our classroom community?
- How could assumptions hurt our community?
- What is the difference between an assumption and a reputation? How are they related?
- Is it easy to change a reputation?
- How could we help if someone wanted to change a reputation?
-
-

(OTHERS)

18

VARIATIONS:

·If you want to save paper and just cut to the chase, use the overhead and discuss each person in the classroom picture. It might even be interesting if the class could come to a consensus about each student.

·Work in pairs. Partners have to come to a consensus about each student in the picture.

·If you have the time, write up a little story about each student in the classroom handout. Use this as the "true" background of each. Make sure to throw a few twists in there to make it interesting.

·Use the following short student histories for added adventure:

From the bottom up. Left to right.

1) Jana has her head buried in the textbook. She is the oldest child in her family and has five more siblings. She is always trying to set a good example for them. Today, under her half smile there is a deep sadness. No matter how hard she tries, it never seems good enough for her parents.

2) Peter likes attention, and goes to great pains to get it. Now he is afraid that he does not have his first day's assignment (a book report on his summer reading) so he is trying to catch Alan's attention. Peter might be able to talk Alan into writing something for him before the teacher calls for his paper. Peter tries to get other students to do his work for him by giving them candy and sodas.

3) Jeff is an only child. Since today is his first day at school, he decided that he does not need any books. He sat on the back row because he does not want anyone to notice that he is sleeping under his sunglasses. He likes to chat online with his friends at night and never gets enough sleep. He is hoping the teacher won't notice.

4) Andrew is a very responsible young man. He is just like his father who died two years ago. He is happy because the teacher seemed to like his book report so far. He thinks this teacher is cool and also very pretty. As for the people in his new class, he is not sure that he is going to like them at all.

5) Sean is an only child from a very wealthy family. He is very intelligent and does not put much effort into anything except trying to rebel and annoy his parents. This is because he spends a great deal of time by himself and feels left out. He just wants attention so he wears crazy clothes and weird colored hair. He thinks that Jana is cute and is wondering how she would look in a purple "mohawk."

6) Gina is writing a letter to her pal from camp. Everyone thinks she is doing class work, but she is catching up with her best friend, Mark, who lives in another state. She is telling Mark about the huge trout she caught a few days ago. She would definitely rather be fishing!

7) Miso is a very pretty Asian girl. She is a high achiever and always does well in school. She can't stop thinking about her mom who is in the hospital. She wants to become a doctor when she grows up because she really likes to help people. She does not have many friends because she lives very far from school and does not

get to hang out with other kids.

8) John is sad because he feels left out. It is not easy being the only black boy in the classroom. He didn't want to come to this school. He liked his old school better, but his mother got a new job and the whole family relocated to a neighborhood across town. He misses his friends.

9) Alan is out of his seat. He is angry at one of his classmates because she borrowed a book before the summer and never returned it. It was a book from the public library so now he is stuck with the late fees. Alan has been in the same school for the past six years. He knows everyone, and he can be a bit arrogant at times.

10) Ed is a "techie." He loves computers more than anything. He is done with his assignment and is now trying to hack his way into the new teacher's files. He is grounded for a month because he dyed his hair black.

11) Jo is a diver, and she broke her legs practicing a jump on a trampoline in her back yard. She hates school, but she loves to browse the web and find out more about her sport. She wants to be in the next Olympic games. She gets up at five every day to practice. This injury is not going to stop her!

OTHER IDEAS:

CLASSROOM

Suppose today is your first day at a new school. You see these kids as you walk into your new classroom. What is your first impression of them? What do you know about each of them? Which of your ideas are facts? Which are opinions?

·--------THOUGHTS · NOTES · REVELATIONS--

CHOSEN

Frank Aycox

POSSIBLE OBJECTIVES: Risk Taking, Observation Skills, Patience, Consensus Building...

NEEDS: No props needed. Area enough for a large circle. The class could be sitting in a circle of desks or sitting on the floor. (Sitting on the floor is better for this observation-type game.)

PROCEDURE: After setting up your circle choose someone from the group that would be willing to be the first "It." You can choose this person before or after you explain the activity. Either choice promotes "Its" own level of risk. "It" observes all the players seated in the circle and asks some of them to stand. Those players selected to stand must have something in common that distinguishes them from those remaining seated. (But, don't tell just yet.) "It" also stands if she has the chosen trait. When seated players want to make a guess, they must raise their hand and be chosen by "It." The first player to answer correctly is the new "It." Mr. Aycox promotes this game as, "an excellent choice for helping students to become more comfortable looking at one another. It promotes an opportunity for students to actually look at peers without being critical." He also says that the more you play this game and the more the students get to know each other, the more sophisticated the trait selections become.

> **NOTE:** This activity is especially challenging when your students wear uniforms. External traits are quickly used up. With this in mind, it might be good to present other activities before this one that will allow your students to get to know about each other; get to know likes and dislikes and the like. Then play CHOSEN, where players choose internal traits - a bit more challenging.

OBSERVATIONS/QUESTIONS:
- What was it like to be the first "It"?
- Was anyone reluctant to be the first "It"? Why?
- What might be some reasons we become reluctant to take risks?
- What kinds of risks might we be taking in this classroom?
- In what ways can we support each other as we take such risks?
- How did you feel when you were asked to stand?
- How did your feelings change as your classmates were observing you?
- Who was willing to make a guess? Who was not?
- How did the group react to the guesses?
- Did those reactions affect anyone?
- Who was involved in the activity? Who was not? Why? Why not?
- Who had ice cream this week?

(OTHERS)
-
-

VARIATIONS:

·Instead of ending after the first correct guess, have "It" choose each person willing to make a guess, and then ask for a consensus to see if the group can agree on a like trait - it might not be the same one "It" chose. (So, is there a right or wrong here?)

·If you are working with a smaller group (time factor), "It" could even ask the standing players what they think the trait might be.

OTHER IDEAS:

LETTER OPENER—
Chris Cavert

POSSIBLE OBJECTIVES: Verbal Communication, Problem Solving, Consensus Building, Decision Making...

NEEDS: Each student will need two 3" x 5" blank index cards and a writing implement - my first choice is always water-based, big tip, markers.

PROCEDURE: The set-up of the room is up to you. If you want to provide another problem to solve, have the desks in rows. See how, and where, the group arranges the cards. Hand out at least two note cards to each student. (You need 30 or more letter cards.) Ask them to write a letter on each card. Make the letter real big. They can write any two letters they wish - but, don't let anyone see just yet.

Here is the challenge: Arrange all the letters into words (words found in a standard diction-ary).
Every word must be attached in some way to another word like in a crossword puzzle. The class is also allowed to change letters - one letter may be changed for every four students in the group, e.g., if there are 20 students, five letters may be changed. Everyone in the class must agree to the letter change. Are there any questions? Go!

OBSERVATIONS/QUESTIONS:
- Did anyone have a hard time choosing letters?
- Why did you choose the letters you did?
- What sort of leadership presented itself during the process? What types of leadership are there?
- Which student or students took on a leadership role? Was their leadership appointed or assumed? Why?
- Did you give up your cards to the process? Why?
- What did you do after you gave up your cards? Did you help?..sit back?..distract?
- Did you hold onto your cards? Why?
- Did you work together to form one large connection of words or did you split into small groups to put words together? How did this work?
- Did you share letters with the other groups?
- How many cards did you change? Was everyone involved in the change?
- What was communication like during the process? Were there communication conflicts?
- What was fun about the activity?

(OTHERS)
-
-

VARIATIONS:

•If you have the prep time (don't laugh, it could happen!), prepare note cards ahead of time. Choose words from a lesson you want to review for. Write a letter from each word on one of the cards. As you hand out two (or maybe three) cards to each student, tell them they are to do the best they can to create words that are related to the subject in review.

OTHER IDEAS:

ASSUMPTION TEST—

POSSIBLE OBJECTIVES: Inclusion, Decision Making, Accepting Diversity, Problem Solving...

NEEDS: You will need a variety of small non-see-through empty containers such as a cereal box, an empty aspirin bottle, a game box, etc. The only limit here will be the space that you have available to set up the test. You will also need a variety of items to put in the containers (read below), a blank sheet of paper and a pencil for each person in the group.

What is in each container?
1.   2.   3   4.   5.   6.   7.

FYI. You will see that the ASSUMPTION TEST requires a lot of props, but I'm guessing that you will not have to "go out" and get any of these items. You should be able to find or borrow containers from your surroundings. Also, I wanted to put this activity in the book because I have had fantastic results with it.

PROCEDURE: Before presenting this test to your group, place an item in each container that is different from what the container advertises. For example, I put beads in the aspirin bottle or macaroni noodles in the cereal box. (If the items you place in the container are similar to what it is supposed to contain, you can shake it giving the class an audio clue.) Set up the containers like the old "Price is Right" game show (I'll bet I just dated myself!) in front of the room - away from the group. When your group arrives and has settled in, hand out a blank piece of paper and a pencil, and tell them they will be taking a test. After the moans and groans, assure them that this is an easy test, and then give them the directions:

1. Please write down, in order from left to right, what the contents of each container is.
2. There will be no talking until everyone is done with this test.

If you get any questions related to the test, try to answer them by repeating the directions. Avoid giving any solutions if problem-solving inquiries are made.

After each person has finished, check the answers. Take the items from their containers one-by-one, opening your own can of worms, so to speak. (That wouldn't be a bad idea – to have a peanut can full of worms as the last item. I've got to write this down. Where's my pencil!)

NOTE: I have had unmitigated success doing this activity with the younger kids - based on the objective I was targeting. Some of the older kids I have tried this with had some experience in the "experiential process" and thought out of the box (they would get up and "look" inside - no rule against that). Nothing wrong with thinking out of the box, it just possibly changes your objective. (We never do that on the run, do we?)

OBSERVATIONS/QUESTIONS:

- What was all the groaning about before the test?
- What has been your experience with tests?
- Was anyone able to guess right on the contents of any container? Why?
- How do you get to know people?
- Do you make an effort to "look inside" of someone before judging them?
- Have you had others judge you before they really got to know you?
- What were the reactions when the contents were revealed?
- Was this a fair test?
- What could you have done to make this test easier for yourself?
- Who got up to look in the containers?
- Did anyone follow their lead? Why? Why not?
-
-

(OTHERS)

VARIATIONS:

- Have something in one of the containers that is supposed to be in there. Sometimes we guess right.
- If you want to really go all out, change the label on a tuna can to a white chicken label. When you get to the can, stop and open up a little discussion (pardon the pun). "Does anyone want to change their answer?" "Will it take a bit more work to see inside this one?" "Does it take more work to see inside of other people?" "Do we give up when things take more work?"

OTHER IDEAS:

THE NUMBER GAME —
John Newstrom, Edward Scannell & McGraw Hill Publishing

POSSIBLE OBJECTIVES: Persistence, Patience, Attention to Task, Accepting Limitations...

NEEDS: Each student will need one copy of THE NUMBER GAME handout and something to write with.

PROCEDURE: Students should be seated at their desk for this one. Place the number sheet face down on each desk. They are not to turn the sheet over until you give instructions to do so. (I have found that there is no advantage gained for students who try to look "through" the back of the sheet. There's an interesting process to explore here. Why are they looking for an advantage?)

Tell the students that this activity is a hand-eye coordination exercise. Have them work independently, without talking, and as fast as they can within the given time period. When you say "Go," players will turn their papers over and locate the number "1" (the only number that is circled on the page) and place their index finger on this number. Then they should look for and place their index finger on the number "2," then find and place their index finger on the number "3" and so on. It is important that they "physically" put their finger on each number before they locate the next number. Continue finding numbers until time is up. Each round will last 60 seconds. When time is up say, "Please stop. Turn your papers over and write the last number you touched on the back of your sheet."

At this point of the game (don't worry there's more) decide how you would like to continue. You can ask everyone to share their numbers with the class (good issues here). You can do a general sharing: "Who made it above 5, 10, 15, 20...?" This way the students can fit "within a group" (issues here). You can also just continue with the next round.

"Get ready for round two." Each round has the same rules - building on previous skills. Always start with the number "1," use the index finger, and count as high as you can in 60 seconds. Repeat this procedure at least six or seven times - I like to do ten rounds if I have the time (oh yes, more issues), and don't forget to write the numbers on the back. When you have completed all the rounds (you and they can possibly stand), it will be time for a little discussion. As customary, I have included some questions.

> NOTE: I have presented this activity over 100 times. More often than not, after the first round, scores will drop for the next round or two. Then the scores tend to go above the first round's score by the end - proving the process that "practice pumps performance" (I think I just made that up). I call this slump the "Learning Wall." We face pressure to constantly improve our performance - especially if we are being graded. Pressure can cause stress, and stress is related to physiological responses of the body. One possible response is a lack of oxygen to the brain. Lack of oxygen to the brain...the "Wall." Some students will give up at the wall,

finding it too difficult to continue. So how can students get over the wall? With some effort. (Encouragement from us sure wouldn't hurt either.) The outcome of anything is the product of effort. If we can demonstate this to our students, the light might turn on. I like to refer back to this activity whenever the group hits the "Wall" at another time. I will ask them what it is that we need right now to get over the "Wall." Please keep in mind that you might have to work through some issues with students who don't get over the "Wall." These students are our opportunity to really teach - OUR "Wall." Just don't forget what effort can do. So I talked your ear off, let's get back to it.

OBSERVATIONS/QUESTIONS:

- What were some feelings you were going through during the activity? Are there times in the classroom when you might feel like this? What can we do to help each other through these feelings?
- What do you think the point of the activity was?
- What was difficult about the activity? How can we relate this to our classroom?
- How many of you experienced the "Wall" during the activity?
- How did/didn't you react to the "Wall"?
- What was the effect of sharing the numbers with the class?
- How did students react to the sharing?
- Did anyone decide to not share her/his numbers?
- Did anyone choose to share an incorrect number? Why do you think this happens?
- Was everyone able to follow the rules?
- Did anyone use both index fingers during the process?
- Did anyone give up? What might be some reasons we give up on something?
- What might be a lesson from this activity?
- Do you want to do a few more rounds!?

(OTHERS)
-
-

VARIATIONS:

- You can also use this activity to work on concentration and relaxation skills. As the time is going down, count off the time remaining every 5 seconds, "55 seconds left, 50 seconds left, 45 seconds left.......10, 9, 8, 7, 6, 5, 4, 3, 2, 1, TIME'S UP!" (Wear eye protection if you decide to try this.) What skills can be learned to help you relax more during/in a distracting environment?
- Turn the sheet upside down - same skills, different look.

OTHER IDEAS:

- The Learning Curve (pg. 33) can be used to plot students' numbers for a visual of their progress (not to mention a little math work).
- THE NUMBER GAME is a good lead into the GROUP NUMBER GAME.

THE NUMBER GAME

Newstrom, John W., Scannell, Edward E., Games Trainers Play, 1980, McGraw Hill, Inc.

LEARNING CURVE

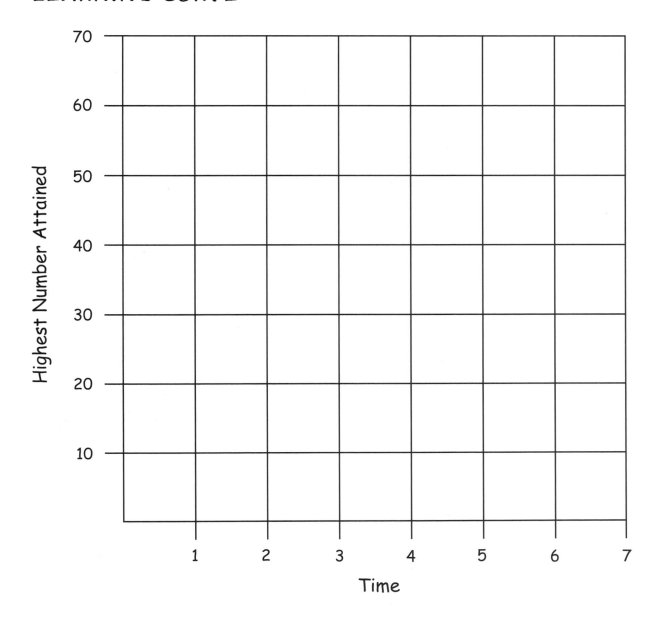

After completing THE NUMBER GAME, have students plot each of their results (sequentially) on the learning curve. Interpolate as needed. Connect each of the seven dots to complete your learning curve. Some possible questions for discussion:

1. Did anyone have an increase every time?
2. Many of us experienced a slight decline or "learning plateau." What might cause this?
3. If we are likely to experience these "plateaus," how can we be more understanding of these situations and adapt to them?

Newstrom, John W., Scannell, Edward E., Games Trainers Play, 1980, McGraw Hill, Inc.

GROUP NUMBER GAME —

POSSIBLE OBJECTIVES: Problem Solving, Verbal Communication, Listening, Inclusion, Consensus Building, Helping, Persistence, Patience, Attention to Task...

NEEDS: Each small group of students will need one copy of the GROUP NUMBER GAME handout and something to write with. You also may want to read THE NUMBER GAME activity if you haven't yet. You can find it on page 29.

PROCEDURE: I find this activity works very well with groups of three. Pairs would be my next choice, then fours. Each group should find a comfortable place to work - on the floor or at desks. Hand out one "number sheet" face down to each group. They are not to turn the sheet over until you give instructions to do so.

Tell the students:
1) This activity is just like THE NUMBER GAME they did at some point back in the year. However, they will be working in small groups to accomplish the same task.

-or-

2) This activity is a hand-eye coordination exercise in which each group will be working as fast as they can to find the numbers on the sheet, in sequential order, within the given time period.

When you say "Go," a player in the group will turn the paper over and locate the number "1" (the only number that is circled on the page), and place their index finger on this number. Then they should look for and place their index finger on the number "2," then find and place their index finger on the number "3" and so on. It is important that they "physically" put their finger on each number before they locate the next number. Continue finding numbers until time is up. Each round will last 60 seconds. When time is up say, "Please stop. Turn your papers over and write this last number you touched on the back of your sheet."

If you have played THE NUMBER GAME and have saved the number handout, compare each student's initial number to the group number they obtained. Any difference? I'll bet you know where this is going?

At this point of the game, you have a choice to share numbers with the class. You can do a general sharing: "Who made it above 5, 10, 15, 20...?" or just continue with the next round. In this number game, I give the groups a 60 second planning between each round - no planning before the first round. Each round has the same rules - building on known skills. Always start with the number "1," use the index finger, and count up as high as you can in 60 seconds. "Go." Repeat this procedure at least six or seven times.

This game is a great way to emphasize the power of groups or in this case, the power of a group this size. (I tried this activity, as an experiment, with a group of 12. One sheet of paper, 12 people - I think you see the picture). SO, some things for some groups.

NOTE: Before you use this activity, consider whether or not your class is ready to work in groups.

OBSERVATIONS/QUESTIONS:
•What were some overall group feelings about this activity? How did you get along? Are there times in a group when you might feel like this? What can we do to help each other through these feelings?
•Was there any leadership in the group? Who?
•Was there too much leadership in the group? How did it affect the process?
•Was leadership necessary?
•What was difficult about the activity? How can we relate this to the group work we will be getting into?
•Did you discover any limits of your group?
•What are some strategies you might use to be more effective during a group project?
•What was the effect of sharing the numbers with the class?
•How did students react to the sharing?
•Was everyone able to follow the rules?
•Did anyone use both index fingers during the process?
•Did anyone give up? What might be some reasons we give up on something?
•What might be a lesson from this activity?
•Rate the effort of your group. What could you have done to get a higher rating?
(OTHERS)
•
•

VARIATIONS:
•You can also use this activity to work on concentration and relaxation skills. As the time is going down, count off the time remaining every 5 seconds, "55 seconds left, 50 seconds left, 45 seconds left.......10, 9, 8, 7, 6, 5, 4, 3, 2, 1, TIME'S UP!" What skills can be learned to relax more during/in a distracting environment?
•After the planning period, do not allow any talking. How does verbal communication affect the process?

OTHER IDEAS:
•THE NUMBER GAME is a good lead into the GROUP NUMBER GAME.

GROUP NUMBER GAME

Newstrom, John W., Scannell, Edward E., Games Trainers Play, 1980, McGraw Hill, Inc.

P.S. —
Chris Cavert

POSSIBLE OBJECTIVES: Problem Solving, Sharing, Listening, Decision Making...

NEEDS: You will need paper (I like to use 5" x 7" cards) and a pencil for each student.

PROCEDURE: This one is really straightforward. Hand out four to six index cards to each student. Have them write the word "problem" on half of their cards, followed by a problem on each problem card they might be facing or any problem they might be aware of. Then have them write the word "solution" on the other half of their cards followed by a possible solution to each of their problems. Make sure the cards stay in order for the first round.

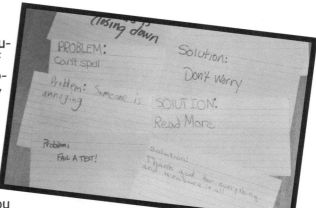

When the students have completed their cards, you can collect them and read them to the class or go around the room and read the cards one at a time. State the problem and then the solution. If time allows, discuss the cards with the group.

At some point (maybe not the same day), try the Mix-and-Match part of the game. Mix all the problems up in one pile and the solutions in another. Then pick a problem and read it. Now pick out a solution. Some of the solutions may be quite funny in comparison to the problem, others might even be a viable option to the problem.

> NOTE: This activity can be used over several sessions. If you don't get to the Mix-and-Match right away, make sure to end your P.S. sessions with something positive so the group will want to continue this activity in the future.

Try to encourage creative answers. Suppose someone writes, "I have a problem swearing too much." Their solution is, "Don't swear." There is nothing in the solution that will modify the behavior. A modifying solution might be, "Give a quarter to the spring party jar every time I swear."

I have also had success using the acronym "P.S." as a signal for someone to look for a solution to a problem they might be getting into at the time - a verbal cue so to speak.

OBSERVATIONS/QUESTIONS:
- What seems to be harder to think of, problems or solutions?
- Did anyone contribute the same problem as another person?
- Has anyone ever tried any of the solutions given? How did they work?
- Why do you think there are so many problems in our lives?
- What can we do to eliminate some of the problems we have?
- Are you able to recognize your own problems?

•How do you react when someone else points out a problem you are having?
•Are you able to try another person's solution to a problem you might be having?

(OTHERS)
•
•

VARIATIONS:

•Carry around the solution cards. When a problem crops up, pick a card to see what happens.
•Write out some problem cards related to things going on in class. Then present the problems to the group and brainstorm possible solutions. Many of my past participants can rattle off many problems but lack appropriate solutions to them.
•Have everyone write a problem card. Gather them, mix them up and pass them out again. Have students write a solution card for the problem card they have been given. Share the problems and then discuss their solutions as time allows. Or play this variation vise versa - start out writing solution cards, followed by figuring out what the problem could be.
•Another fun card resource I like to use for problem solving is the "*Creative Whack Pack,*" by Roger von Oech. The pack includes 64 cards consisting of different problem solving strategies and ideas. You can find the pack at most of your local book stores.
•Get together in small groups to discuss/brainstorm solutions to problem cards.

OTHER IDEAS:

SIMPLY PAPER —
Craig Dobkin

POSSIBLE OBJECTIVES: Accepting Diversity, Accepting Limitations, Sharing...

NEEDS: Each student will need a blank 8 1/2" by 11" sheet of paper and a writing implement - I like to use crayons or water-based markers for some color (the spice of life).

PROCEDURE: Students can do this activity right at their desks. I prefer to put the desks in a big circle so the sharing works out a little better, but any desk configuration will work (well okay, maybe not any). Don't hesitate (as with any of the activities in this book) to play this one yourself. It's a good way to show your students that no matter how old we might be, new things are challenging. Bridging the gap can always be useful.

PHASE 1)
Hand out a piece of paper to each student and approve their writing tool of choice (you might want to stay away from the "sharper" writing tools - you'll see). Ask your students to write their full name on the paper - but, the catch is this: they must write on the paper while it is on their forehead (this is where the sharp writing tool might be a problem). After the moans and groans, encourage them to do the best they can. When everyone in the class has completed the task, share the results.

> NOTE: If you do some processing here, ask the students not to re-configure or add to the paper in any way because they will need to use it again.

OBSERVATIONS/QUESTIONS (PHASE 1):
- What was the reaction to the activity?
- In what situations do we seem to react the same way? Why?
- Did you write big or small? Why?
- We all know how to write our names, why was this a challenge? How is this like school?
- Did everyone do the best that they could? What is important about this?
- How did your writing turn out?
- Do you think you could do better? What would it take?
- Let's try another challenge?

(OTHERS)
-
-

PHASE 2)

With papers flat on their desks, using the same side of the paper as their forehead hand writing, ask students to write their full name again. This time write with their non-dominant hand. When everyone has finished, share the results.

OBSERVATIONS/QUESTIONS (PHASE 2):

- What was the reaction to this phase? Why was it different?
- How was this phase compared to the first?
- How do the two signatures differ?
- Has anyone ever had to use their non-dominant hand for a long period of time? How was your writing?
- Have everyone write their full name on the paper as they normally would. How do the three attempts compare? Alike? Different? Why?
- Did anyone compare their work with the work of others? Why?
- How about another challenge?
-
-

(OTHERS)

PHASE 3)

Ask the students to sit across from another person in the classroom - a group of three will work. When the shuffling is done, ask them to turn their papers over to the blank side (we hope it's blank). Give them 15 seconds to study the facial features of their partner. Then, with eyes shut, ask them to draw their partner to the best of their ability. When everyone has finished, share the results.

OBSERVATIONS/QUESTIONS (PHASE 3):

- How was this phase for you?
- What were some of the thoughts you were having during this activity?
- If I said you were going to be graded on this activity, how would it change?
- How did your partner react to your drawing?
- Can you draw? Are you an artist? When did you decide this? Did you decide, or did someone else decide this for you?
- Did you do the best that you could?
- What might be some important lessons from the three phases of this activity?
- How can we implement these lessons in our classroom? In school? At home?
- Was this activity fun? Why? Why not?
-
-

(OTHERS)

VARIATIONS:

OTHER IDEAS:

·Craig likes to use this same piece of paper and progress into YOU TEAR ME UP.
·You could also save this paper and use it for CHALLENGE FIELD, CHRIS-CROSS,
COMMUNITY BOX or DON'T SPILL THE BEANS.

EMPATHY—

POSSIBLE OBJECTIVES: Sharing, Verbal Communication, Decision Making, Accepting Diversity...

NEEDS: Cut out the Noun Cards included in this activity and place them in a bowl or a hat - something the students can reach in to pick out a card. You're ready to go.

PROCEDURE: This activity can be done with just about any room set-up. As you know, my favorite is the circle formation. When everyone is ready, have one of the students volunteer to pick out a Noun Card. You can ask the student to stand by their desk or at the front of the room. Each involves a different level of risk. Let the group know what was chosen. Then ask the player who picked the card a question from the list provided below. Have them answer as if they are the noun on their card.

> What is your favorite food?
> What is your favorite thing to do?
> Where is your favorite place to go?
> What do others say when they make fun of you? How do you feel about that?
> What do people say to make you happy?
> What do people say to make you sad?
> What do people say to make you angry?
> What do people say to make you proud?
> What do people say to make you confident?

That is the basic implementation of the activity. Now, there are several ways to go from here:

A. You can ask the same person who chose the card each one of the questions in order over the same Noun Card.
B. Use the same Noun Card and ask a different student one of each of the questions.
C. Each student chooses one Noun Card and is asked one question.
D. Each player answers the question in relation to the Noun Card that is being played, and for themselves, e.g., Frog - what is a frog's favorite thing to do? You - what is your favorite thing to do?
E. Write the questions on 3" x 5" note cards (one question on each card). After students pick a Noun Card they could also pick a question to answer. Put both Noun and Question cards back in the pile.

No matter how you present this activity, always provide the option to pass. If someone passes, open the question up to the class to see if anyone else wants to answer it.

OBSERVATIONS/QUESTIONS:

• What was it like to be in someone/something else's shoes? Easy? Difficult? Why?

•Can we really be in someone else's shoes (well, we literally could, but don't go there)?
•What might be helpful about being in someone else's shoes?
•Did anyone pass on a question? Why?
•Who struggled with the questions? What were you thinking about?
•What sorts of interaction have you had with our nouns in the past? How might these interactions affect your answers?
•If you had never interacted with the nouns, what information were you drawing from to answer the questions? Is this the best source? What is the best source?
•What nouns would you add to the list?

(OTHERS)

•

•

VARIATIONS

•Have a small group pick nouns and have another small group ask the questions. The group that chooses the noun will have to come up with an answer, by consensus, within 60 seconds.

OTHER IDEAS:

Frog	Rock
Short Person	Tall Person
Heavy Person	Thin Person
Star Athlete	Dirt
Tomato	Bathtub

White Person

Native American Person

Black Person

Asian Person

Physically Handicapped Person

Weather Person

Hearing Impaired Person

Strong Person

Weak Person

Me

BLUE CARDS ━━

POSSIBLE OBJECTIVES: Sharing, Decision Making, Support, Accepting Feedback...

NEEDS: I like to use blue, 3" x 5" note cards (goes along with the name). You will need one card for each person in your class. Write the names of your students on the cards – one name per card. (You can put your name on a card, too. We all need those blue cards!) You're ready to go.

PROCEDURE: I got the idea for the name of this activity from a famous educator of the 80s era (his name escapes me, but his thoughts are still imprinted in my mind). His premise is that our children receive too many "red cards" - negative comments - during the day. We need to give out more "blue cards" - positive comments - if we want to help our children feel better about themselves and what they do. So, here is the opportunity to get a "blue card" in there.

With my blue cards in hand (there's a name on every one), I say, "It's time for a blue card." I pass out a card to every student in the class. Then I ask them to say something nice about the person that is listed on their card. As the leader you can pick students one at a time, or let the students stand up on their own. Make sure everyone receives some feedback. If one of your students is having a really hard time with this process, collect his card and ask if anyone would be willing to do two cards. Remember, if you build trust through challenge-by-choice (giving them the option of pass or play), in a supportive environment, most people will end up playing. If a student receives their own name, they must share something they are proud of about themselves or pass the card up for someone to help out.

My presentation of this activity changes throughout the year. During the beginning of the year, I let students sit at their desks. I also let them say superficial things like, "I like the shirt you're wearing," or "You have a nice smile." (We will spend some discussion time on feedback as well, using some of the questions below.) As the year progresses however, I like to make things a bit more challenging. I will ask them to stand by their desk, look at the person they are addressing, and use the person's name within the feedback they are giving. I will also ask the person receiving the feedback to say "thank you" to the person giving it. This part encourages students to accept/acknowledge feedback. (Sometimes this is even harder than giving it.)

I may also ask students to "complete the sentence" I give out. For example:

> (Person's name) thank you for...
> (Person's name) I like the way you...
> (Person's name) is really good at...
> (Person's name) is going to...
> I was surprised to find out that...
> I didn't know that...

47

This activity really helps the students to be more aware of each other and what they are doing. If it's "blue card time," they want to be ready. Also, teaching students how to talk to each other and give each other feedback will help them to relate to each other in more positive ways.

OBSERVATIONS/QUESTIONS:

- Is it easy/hard for you to give other people feedback? Why is this?
- Is it easy/hard for you to accept feedback? Why is this?
- Is feedback negative or positive?
- What might be important about feedback?
- What sorts of feedback do we use in this class? How is it helpful? When can it be harmful?
- What are some good ways to give someone feedback?
- Can anyone give some examples of bad ways to give feedback?
- Is it easier to give positive or negative feedback? What do we hear more? What would we like to hear more? Why?
- Is there another person in the class you would like to give feedback to?
- How do you feel about giving feedback to an adult? Have you ever been able to do this? How did it turn out?
- What sort of feedback would you give to some of the adults in your life? (You could do a feedback box for this one and discuss the comments.)

(OTHERS)
-
-

VARIATIONS:

- Have an open "blue card" day. Anyone in the class can stand up and give anyone else some positive feedback.

OTHER IDEAS:

PENCIL, PAPER, POPSICLE STICK —
Adapted from Knapp's Communication Patterns Activities.

POSSIBLE OBJECTIVES: Problem Solving, Listening, Verbal Communication, Decision Making, Accepting Limitations...

NEEDS: For each pair of group members you will need two identical pieces of paper, two similar pencils, and two matching popsicle sticks.

PROCEDURE: The only preparation that takes a little time is coloring the sticks (I have some sudents help me the day before – using markers). Make sure that every two sticks have the same colored patterns on them; the pairs of sticks do not have to match other pairs.

This is a good activity for understanding directions and how they can be misunderstood. When you're ready, creatively pair up group members. Give each player in the pair half of a matching set of the above gear: one piece of paper, one pencil and one popsicle stick. Have the partners sit back-to-back on the floor. Have each pair decide who will be the leader for the first round. The leader starts by arranging the three items in a pattern on the floor in front of him, and then attempts to describe the arrangement to his or her partner. The partner is not allowed to speak or look around during the activity. When completed, have the partners look at each others' patterns. If you think it is needed, ask a few questions, but don't completely process until after each player has been a leader. Switch roles and repeat the activity. I like to time this activity to keep transitions consistent.

OBSERVATIONS/QUESTIONS:
- How did you do?
- Did the patterns turn out the same? Why or why not?
- How did leaders feel when they saw their partner's patterns.
- Where did problems arise between partners?
- Did you and your partner figure out a way to communicate nonverbally?
- Was it easy to follow the rules of the task?
- What would the task have been like if you could have asked questions?
- Would asking questions help you do a better job?
- How would asking questions help the leader do a better job?
- What is important about asking questions?
- What tends to happen if we don't ask questions when we're confused?
- How can we make it easy to ask questions in our classroom?
- (OTHERS)
-

VARIATIONS:

· If there is time, repeat the activity and allow partners to talk.
· Add more matching objects.
· Give each person five or six building blocks. Have the leader build and describe a sculpture.

OTHER IDEAS:

PARTICULARS —

POSSIBLE OBJECTIVES: Attention to Task, Decision Making, Accepting Failure, Consensus Building, Persistence, Problem Solving...

NEEDS: Paper and pencil for each student is the first step. The rest of the activity involves changing items on your desk. So, you'll need a desk and a bunch of items on it - read on for more particulars.

PROCEDURE: This activity focuses on the particular skill of observation to detail. I'm going to assume that you have a desk. Most of the desks I've seen have a good deal of "stuff" on them (as well as in them). If you are a person who likes to keep her desk top clear of "stuff," then gather a few things from your room and place them about the top of your desk. The number of items you plan to use might depend on the age of your class.

The basic idea here is to have the students observe the particular items on your desk for one minute. They are not allowed to write down anything or draw anything on their paper - no Polaroids® either. I usually have the students stay at their own desk during this activity. There are some interesting issues to discuss in this area.

After the minute is up, ask the students to put their heads down on their own desk, keeping their eyes away from your desk - closing their eyes would be a nice added challenge. Now you have to change some particulars on your desk. As I said before, the number of things you change might depend on the age group you are working with. There is a bit of a challenge in this for you as well. When you change the items, you have to remember what you changed so you are able to confirm your students' answers. The more I change, the harder it is for me to remember - you might have a better short-term memory than I do! The best suggestion I can make in this area is a little prior planning. Before your students arrive for the day, write a list of the items on your desk down the left side of a piece of paper, then write the changes you are going to make down the right side (not everything on your desk needs to be changed - but you knew that). You're ready for the quick switch.

You have a chance to practice this yourself. Get a half sheet of paper ready - you bet, right now. Turn to page 53 and cover up the bottom picture. Study the top picture for 60 seconds. Now move the paper covering the bottom picture over the top picture. Can you find ten changes in the bottom picture?

OBSERVATIONS/QUESTIONS:
   •Did anyone discover all the particular changes?
   •How many changes did each one of you find? Is this good or bad? (It is neither, it just is – my favorite contemplation.)
   •What was the most difficult part of this activity?
   •How did your place in the room affect your success?
   •What could you add to this activity to make it more successful for you - besides looking while the teacher is making the changes? (Note taking?)

•Did anyone ask for help from another classmate? Why? Why not?
•Was there any discussion in the room?
•Did I say, during the directions, that you couldn't discuss anything?
•Did anyone ask the teacher for help?
•What might be important about asking for help?
•Why do you think we have a hard time asking for help?
•How could we make it easier to ask for help in this classroom?
•
•

(OTHERS)

VARIATIONS:

•Change one item at a time. When the class is ready for a guess, have them come to a consensus on the item changed before giving you their guess.
•To emphasize the benefits of practice, do this activity in several rounds. After the first round, have the students put their heads back down on the desk. Put your desk back into the original layout. Ask the students to observe the desk again, for one minute. Put the heads back down, change the desk, observe the changes. How many times does it take for everyone to find all the changes? Are the students who need more time for this activity the same students who need more time in other areas of study?
•For the "global particular" version, change things around the room!
•Have the students watch as you make changes - no writing while you change. Now how many particular changes can they get right? This one is really interesting.

OTHER IDEAS:

PARTICULARS PICTURES

Cover the bottom picture. Study the top picture for 60 seconds. Move the paper covering the bottom picture over the top picture. Can you find ten changes on the bottom desk?

ROOMINATION —

POSSIBLE OBJECTIVES: Verbal Communication, Accepting Feedback, Problem Solving, Consensus Building, Compromising, Cooperation...

NEEDS: Each small group will need a copy of the grid sheet provided or a large piece of white paper. Something to draw with would also be very helpful.

PROCEDURE: A consideration you might want to ponder before you split your class up into groups is how many times you are willing to redecorate the contents of your room. If you like the room just the way it is, consider this a hypothetical situation or choose a variation below that might suit your needs better.

When you have divided your students up into small groups, hand them the supplies you are providing. You can go so far as to create paper furniture similar to the classroom furniture and a large sheet of paper that resembles the shape of the room (a nice math project on 'scale'). I've also found it helpful to provide extras for draft proposals.

The objective of the activity is for each group to come up with a new room plan using all the furnishings in the room. They can add reasonable fixtures (to your discretion of course - obtaining them is also another issue) but, unless possible, nothing can be removed (I know how busy our maintenance engineers can get). All the groups should consider things like: work areas, personal space, comfort, distractions, teaching space, presentation space, moving about the room, communication issues, safety, etc.

Inform the groups that all designs will be considered for ROOMINATION - that is, actually rearranging the room to the specifications of the designs. As the teacher you will want to decide how long the room will stay the new way. I find it best to give each roomination the same amount of time. As the instructor, you have the final say as to what will or will not work. (Make sure that when you roominate the group who proposed the change does the physical work of moving the room!)

When all the groups have finished, have them share their design and get feedback from the class and teacher. If there is some additional time, groups can get together again to consider some of the information they received. They can add to, change or keep what they have for their final submission.

I like this activity because it gets students invested in their surroundings. They tend to learn what is helpful and what might not be helpful in a learning environment. I also really like the room change now and again.

OBSERVATIONS/QUESTIONS:
- How did you feel about the group you were working with?
- What were some ways that you got organized?
- What sort of leadership developed during the activity?

•Was everyone in your group involved in the process? Why? Why not?
•How did you contribute to the process?
•What went well for your group?
•What problems came up? How did you solve the problems?
•Did everyone finish in the time allotted? Why? Why not?
•How did you take the feedback your classmates gave you?
•What would be something important about feedback?
•Were you able to use any of the advice the class gave you?
•How would you grade your layout based on the criteria given?
•Which room layout is the best? How do you choose the "best" of something?
•How could we choose the order of Roomination?

(OTHERS)
•
•

VARIATIONS:

•If you do not want to change the room, what about re-designing a bulletin board or a classroom wall.
•Small groups could also design their own school. It's fun to see what areas of study get the most space.
•If you have a small group, or the time, have each student draw a layout on grid paper of their current study area at home. Then draw a different study area they would consider to be "state of the art." (This has given me a chance to see [figuratively] where the students study and allows me a way to give them some feedback on how to improve their study area if needed.)

OTHER IDEAS:

Roomination Grid

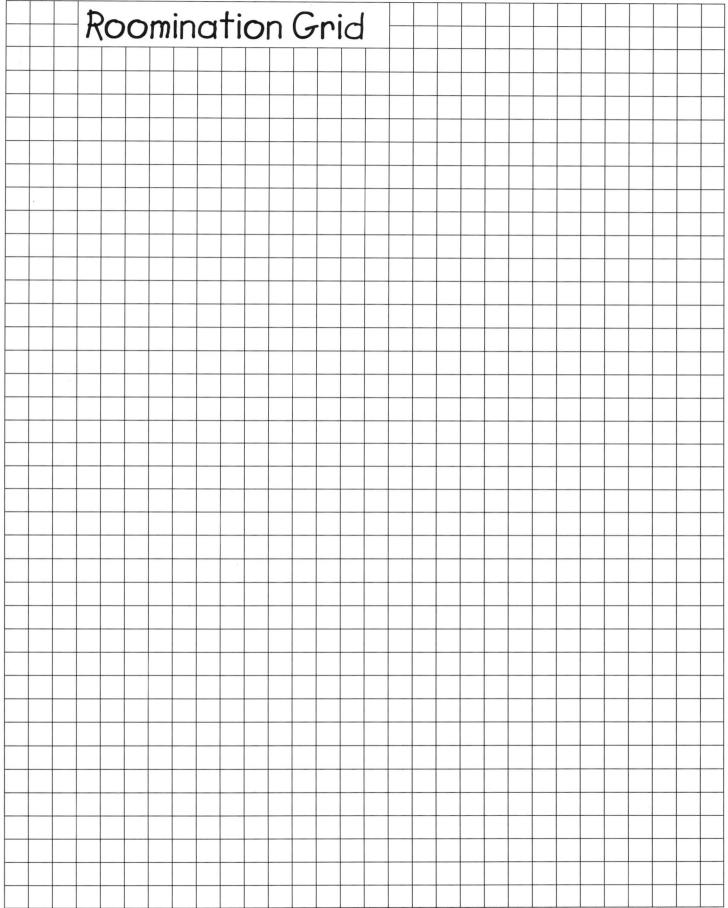

----------THOUGHTS · NOTES · REVELATIONS--

ENUMERATING —

POSSIBLE OBJECTIVES: Verbal Communication, Sharing, Listening, Consensus Building, Compromising...

NEEDS: Each small group will need a blank sheet of paper and a pencil.

PROCEDURE: Split your students up into small groups of three to five people. (This might be a good activity to try before heading into a small group project.) Ask the groups to sit together somewhere in the room.

The second step will be for each group to pick a secretary. When each group has a secretary, give this person a blank sheet of paper and a pencil.

Next, have someone from the group, other than the secretary, come up to you and choose a topic card - pick from a hat or bowl. I have included some cards that you can copy and cut out, or feel free to make up your own cards. You could do school subjects or lessons that the students could review.

After the topic makes its way back to the group, ask the students to enumerate (list) as many things as they can think of that fit within the topic they chose. I'll bet you know who is supposed to write everything down? Give the students five to ten minutes. I watch for the energy level, and when it starts to run low, I'll call a three-minute warning. In this last three minutes each group must decide the top three most important items or people they wrote down. The group must reach consensus on all three items. (If groups need a little more time, you can run over a bit.)

When the time is up, ask each group to choose a speaker - not the secretary. When there is a speaker for each group, they will take turns reporting on:

    1. What category did you have?
    2. How many items/people did you brainstorm?
    3. What were your top three picks?
    4. How did your group choose its secretary and speaker?

After everyone has reported, one of the possible topics to discuss could be the methods for choosing people for roles of responsibility, and how each method may or may not work.

OBSERVATIONS/QUESTIONS:
    •What is brainstorming? How can this be helpful?
    •What challenges did your group face?
    •Was everyone involved in the process? Why? Why not?
    •Did anyone volunteer to be the secretary? Speaker?
    •When you chose a secretary, did you think this person had to be a girl? Why?
    •How did your group decide if there was more than one volunteer?

·How did you feel about being/not being picked? How did you perform your task?
·What is peer pressure? Is it good? Bad? Can it be helpful?
·How was the secretary and speaker treated?
·How do you feel about standing in front of your peers and talking?
·Was there leadership in the group? How was the leader chosen?
·Is it necessary to have leadership during a group project?
·What sorts of leadership are there?
·What type of leadership are you more likely to follow?
·What was your top choice from the list?
·
·

(OTHERS)

VARIATIONS:

·Every group could have the same topic. How many total items or people can be enumerated? Could the entire class come to a consensus on the number one item or person?

OTHER IDEAS:

People	Famous People
Actors/ Actresses	Politicians
Hand Tools	School Supplies
Games	Flowers
Moving Objects	Non-Moving Objects

House Pets	Musical Instruments
Technology Gadgets	Book Characters
Movie/TV Characters	Furniture
Appliances	Slimey Things
Designer Labels	Sports Persons

(See p. 46 for blank topic cards to fill in as needed.)

CLASSROOM POETRY—
Jackie Gerstein

POSSIBLE OBJECTIVES: Sharing, Listening, Verbal Communication, Consensus Building, Compromising, Cooperation...

NEEDS: Make a copy of the Classroom Poetry Cards and cut them out - don't forget, kids love to help. (If you have the resources to laminate these cards, they will last for more than a couple of uses.) You will also need a piece of paper and a pencil for each group.

PROCEDURE: You will want to make small groups depending on the size of your class. Each group should have no less than five poetry cards. So, if you have a small class each student could work individually. I usually don't put any more than three in a group for this one. Bottom line – put together groups of one to three players. It is all up to you and the goals you have in mind. Also, you don't have to use all the cards.

Here's how it works. Ask the groups to find a comfortable place in the room – on the floor or at a cluster of desks. One member from each group should aquire from you the number of cards they will be using (five to eight cards is good), and then return to their group. Here's how you explain it:

"Each card has words on it. Your task (as an individual or group) is to integrate the words on the cards with your own words in order to make a poem. Your own words can be used as deemed necessary. You may also change the tense of the words on the cards, i.e., from past to present and/or from singular to plural. The poem does not have to rhyme."

Each group should first choose a secretary who will write down ideas and the final poem. At this point they are free to create.

You can set a time for this one if you need to. I like to observe the processes of each group and end when groups have completed all the work. If any group finishes early, provide them with more cards and have them create another poem.

Sharing time is always the best part of this activity for me. Ask someone in the group (other than the secretary) to stand and share the final masterpiece with the rest of the class. Keep your professional eye open for any issues that might be in or between the lines of the poems. Always good things to talk about.

OBSERVATIONS/QUESTIONS:
- How were the groups formed? Why?
- How did your group decide who was going to get the cards?
- How did your group choose a secretary?
- What sort of leadership did your group have?
- What kinds of leadership could groups use during a project?
- What leadership style works best for you?
- What roles did each person play in the group?

•Did everyone in the group participate?
•Was everyone able to contribute something to the final project?
•What was difficult about the activity? How did you overcome the challenge?
•What does consensus mean? What does it take to reach consensus?
•Was your group able to reach consensus?
•What do you think is important about consensus?
•When do you think we could use consensus within our classroom?
•
•

(OTHERS)

VARIATIONS:

•When presenting the poem, have each group stand up. Each group member can present one or two lines from the final work.
•Provide some additional construction paper and a glue stick. Have each group write words and glue cards onto the construction paper. Now you can hang the finished products around the room.

OTHER IDEAS:

POETRY CARDS

in the middle of the classroom	a note making its way across the rows
silently taking notes from the board	laughing at the student with a lisp
the teacher said	her heart was broken
it is good to see him smile	with a confident stride
in a soft voice	a loud crash that startled everyone
running toward the window	along the busy halls

GAMES (& other stuff) FOR TEACHERS, © 1999 CHRIS CAVERT/WOOD 'N' BARNES PUBLISHING & DISTRIBUTION

POETRY CARDS (con't)

from one classroom to the next	the sun filtering through the windows
their arms brushed softly against each other	like monkeys, wild with excitement
nobody seemed to care	patiently waiting my turn
the younger students marched quietly down the hall	with his mouth full of food
taking a short break	the book fell noisily to the ground
in between first and second period	a lovely voice reading slowly to us

POETRY CARDS (con't)

all talking at the same time	the intercom broke down
danced in the gym	sad and without friends
in groups of two or three	enjoying our free time
a chair fell over	in the sleepy time after lunch
many of her friends ran to the bleachers	the ball bounced one too many times
bored out of his mind	nothing comes from nothing

POETRY CARDS (con't)

little shiny particles of dust floating in the sun	like made for one another
strawberry blonde hair	I was the first in line
a very rude comment	every other day
not knowing where to go	everyone burst out laughing hysterically
he did not like Mondays	falling in love for the first time
they thought he was in trouble	like "a" is for apple, and "b" is for book

POETRY CARDS (con't)

sunny, happy faces	the teams were very tired
we realized that 2+2 is <u>not</u> always 4	it's all a matter of perception
she thinks she's very popular	strong arms to carry desks around
busy, busy, always busy	understanding and fun teacher
"Good morning," she said	always attentive
after a horrible lunch	looking directly in her eyes

POETRY CARDS (con't)

just standing there	with the desks in a big circle
like a cloud over his head	I care about you
crying in the restroom	caught the ball in mid-air
jump up and down	absolutely wild
we started with great enthusiasm	went to the principal's office
but the janitor was there	silly, giggly students

GAMES (& other stuff) FOR TEACHERS, © 1999 CHRIS CAVERT/WOOD 'N' BARNES PUBLISHING & DISTRIBUTION

POETRY CARDS (con't)

"Always number one," said Dad	the pencil broke in half
a blob of ink on the desk	food fight in the lunchroom
it felt like her first day at a new school	shutting his locker on his finger
listening to the music in her head	I need to sharpen my pencil
my dog ate my homework	he is the teacher's pet
he fell asleep and drooled on his desk	she felt sick and dizzy

GAMES (& other stuff) FOR TEACHERS, © 1999 CHRIS CAVERT/WOOD 'N' BARNES PUBLISHING & DISTRIBUTION

POETRY CARDS (con't)

IT'S ALL IN THE CARDS —
Scott Trent

POSSIBLE OBJECTIVES: Problem Solving, Verbal Communication, Cooperation, Sharing, Consensus Building...

NEEDS: You will need to copy a set of LSN (letter, shape, & number) cards. If you have more than 25 students in your class (I'm sorry), copy some blank cards and fill them in – circles and squares are the numbers; diamonds and triangles are the letters. You will also want a stop watch of some kind.

PROCEDURE: Open up a nice large space in your room to play. You already know my favorite place is an open space in the middle of the room, but there are other arrangements. (If you can get outside for this one, go for it!) Have the students gather in the void. Give each student a LSN card. Tell the students you will be timing the rounds of this activity. Encourage them to do the best that they can and be play safe. You know the old saying, "It's better to be safe than have to explain to your parents that you were fooling around and you ran into a desk." The following is my standard progression of instructions. Feel free to adapt it to your situation.

1. Line up in a circle (yes, a circle is a line) by the order of numbers in the circles. Go.
2. Line up in a circle by the order of the letters in the diamonds. Ready? Go.
3. Line up in a circle by the order of the numbers in the squares. Ready? Go.
4. Line up in a circle by the order of the letters in the triangles. Ready? Go.

Asking the group if they are "ready" provides an opportunity for them to ask you for time to plan a strategy. Many groups will not speak up and ask for time. So, what can they learn from this?

OBSERVATIONS/QUESTIONS:
- Was there any leadership in the beginning? Did it change as you progressed?
- How did the times compare? Why were they different/same?
- Was anyone not ready when one of the rounds started? Did you say anything?
- Was there any planning before any of the rounds?
- What happened during the planning? Was it helpful?
- Was everyone clear on what was happening?
- How did you decide what was going to be done? Force? Consensus? Compromise?
- How would you grade the progress of this group?

•What are some things we learned here that we could use, or not use, in class?
•
•

If you have the time to continue (or you could do this another day), move into this interactive-consensus-commonalities activity. Ask students to pair up (you can make a group of three if needed) by matching cards in some way using the letters and numbers, e.g., a number two can be matched with a number one or a number three. Ask the pairs, when attached, to find something they have in common. (Encourage going beyond the superficial commonalties.) Go around the room, and ask each pair how they are attached and what they have in common. Move on to matching in groups of three (encourage them to leave their original partner). What do these three have in common? Groups of 4, 5, 6...you get the idea. You can form any size group your time allows for. This activity provides an opportunity for some good social interaction. I'll leave the processing up to you on this one.

VARIATIONS:
•Add another challenge to the first four steps (good for advanced minds). Line up in the shape. "Line up in a square by the order of the numbers in the square."
•What about this for crazy. "Line up in a diamond shape by the order of the letters in the triangle!"

OTHER IDEAS:
(These cards come from Scott Trent's "Building Block" system. The letters, shapes and numbers are laser imprinted on 2" x 6" x 9" wooden blocks that Mr. Trent uses for a wide variety of activities. Check out the Reference page for more information. I would have to put this block system up in the highly educational level.)

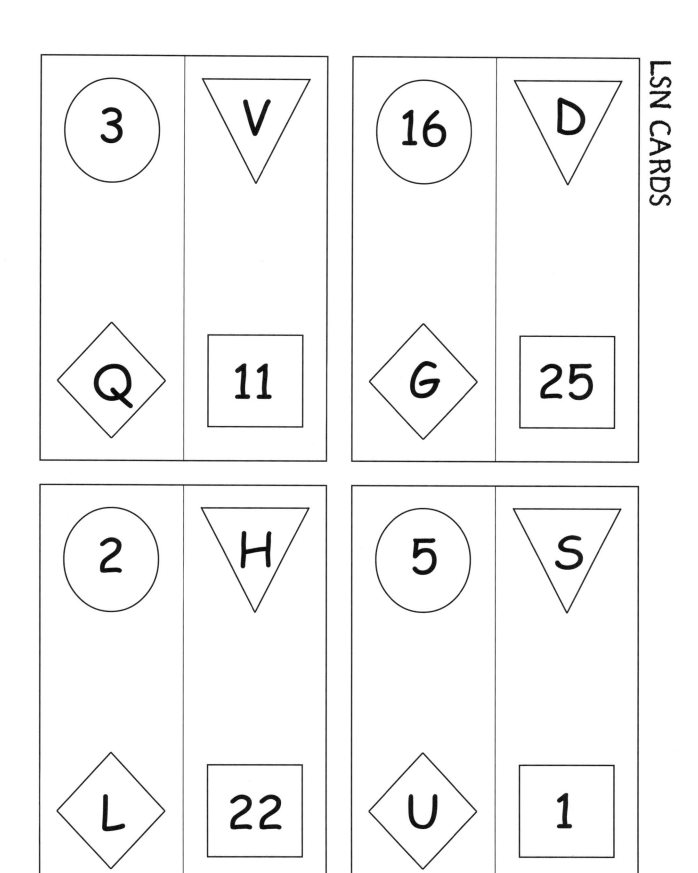

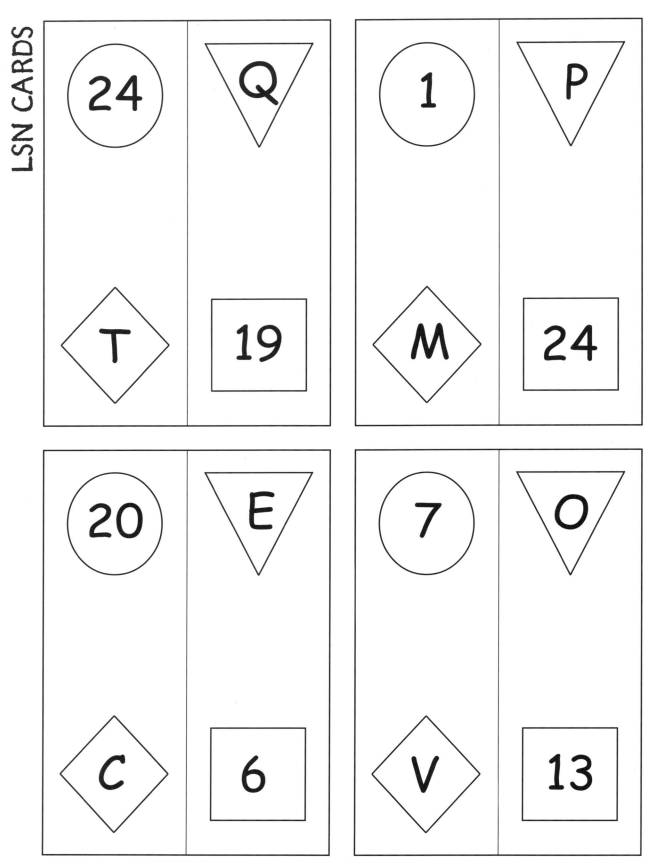

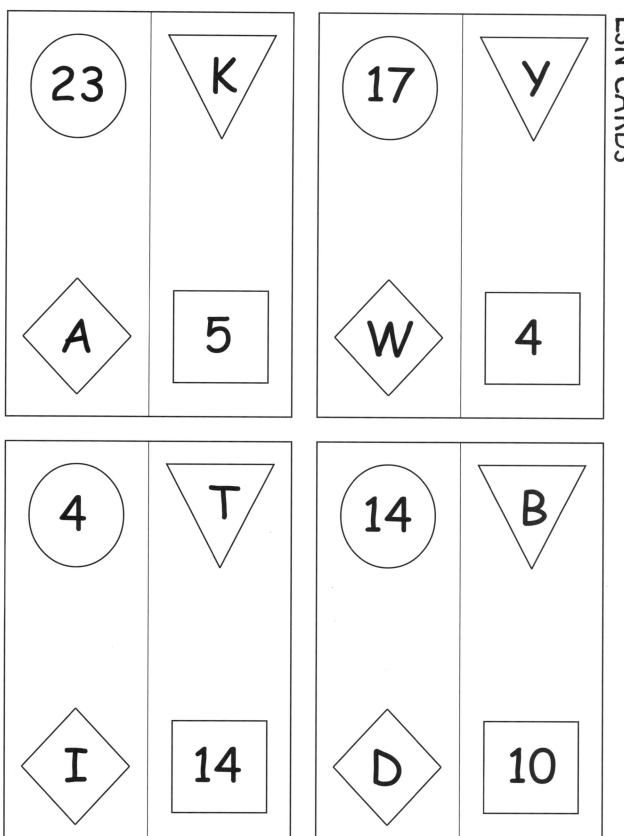

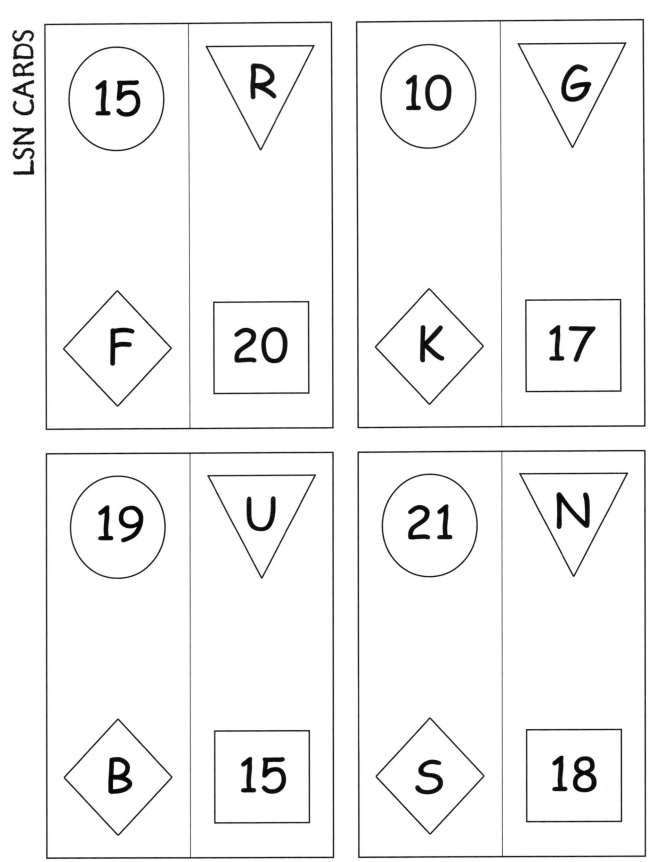

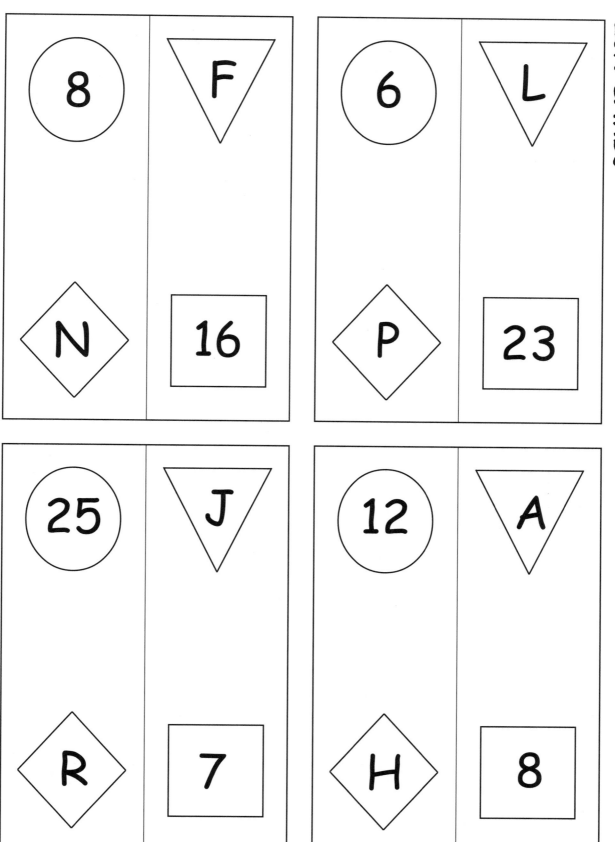

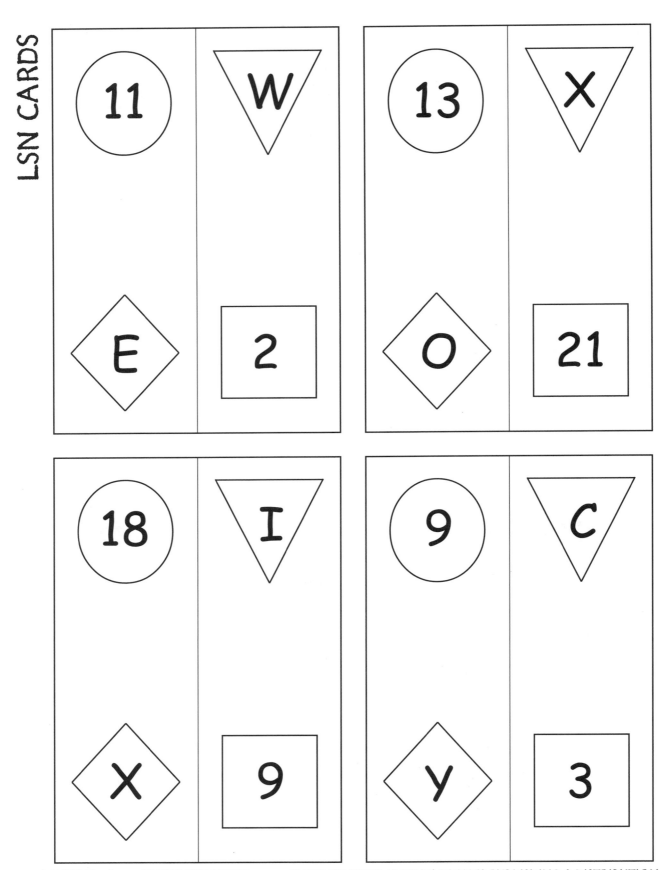

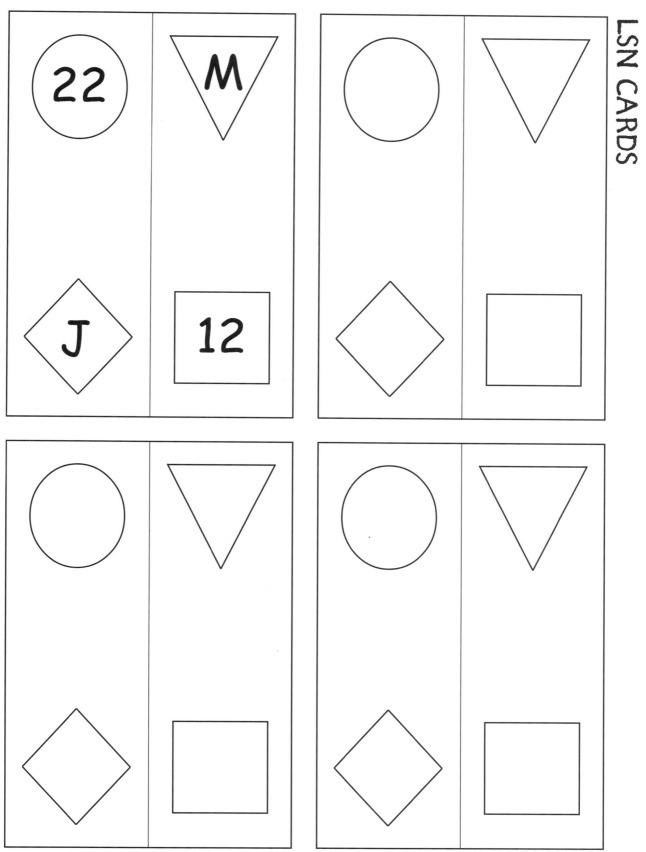

--GAMES for TEACHERS----------

--------THOUGHTS · NOTES · REVELATIONS--

CIRCLE-A-LOONS—
Karl Rohnke

POSSIBLE OBJECTIVES: Persistence, Attention to Task, Problem Solving...

NEEDS: The all out version of this one requires a balloon for each player, but if you can only find one, that's all you really need. Keep in mind that if you only have one balloon and it breaks, your game is over! So what am I really saying here? You need a bunch of balloons!

PROCEDURE: Organize your group in a circle. There are a number of options here. Sitting on the floor facing center, sitting in chairs facing center, standing in a circle facing center, or standing in a circle facing front-to-back with every player's left shoulder directed toward the center of the circle.

When your circle is set, here is the objective: A fully inflated balloon must be passed through the legs of each person in the circle starting and ending with the same person. So let's look at the circle formations we mentioned above. When sitting on the floor, players will have one leg flat on the floor, the other bent at the knee to create a hole for the "loon" to go through. If sitting in a chair, a player's feet must be apart in some manner so the loon can pass through. Standing, facing center would be the same as sitting in a chair – feet have to be apart. When standing front-to-back, the balloon is passed (football hike style) through the legs.

Seem easy? Let's put the Rohnke challenge to it. "Each person is allowed one-half second for the passage [of the loon] between their legs." Let's do the math. If you have 12 people in your group, they have six seconds to get the loon around the circle, starting and ending with the same player. Yes, we are setting the goal for them. We are challenging their abilities. We are dangling a carrot in front of them. We are...aren't we? In any case, can they do it? Yes, if they work together.

NOTE: I like to include myself in this one if the group can allow me to play without helping with the problem-solving challenges. I have also used this activity to role-model play-appropriate problem-solving and communication skills. I will go through the S.O.D.A.S. steps for problem-solving. Look at the SITUATION we are facing. Discuss possible OPTIONS. Evaluate the DISADVANTAGES and the ADVANTAGES of each option. Finally, choose a SOLUTION we would be willing to try. A somewhat long process to learn, but one that becomes more natural with practice.

OBSERVATIONS/QUESTIONS:
•Were you successful? Why? Why not?
•What is cooperation? Was every player cooperating?

•How can cooperating with others help you? Help others?
•Was anyone in the group not cooperating? What was the result?
•How were we communicating during the activity?
•In what ways could we improve our communication?
•What sort of situations did you encounter?
•How were you able to solve the negative situations?
•Was there any leadership taking place? Was it helpful?
•What would you do differently if you were able to try this again?
•
•

(OTHERS)

VARIATIONS:

•For a nice easy start, see how fast the group can pass/hand off the balloon around the circle – not going through legs. Each player has to touch the balloon.
•You might want to let the group determine how long it will take them to get the balloon around the circle. Then you could challenge them with the one-half second each.
•Karl suggests a variation where each player has a balloon with their name on it. Players start with their own balloon. Each balloon must go around the circle back to its original person before the timer stops.
•How about not suggesting any of the circle formation options. Or mention nothing about a circle. Just give them the directions, eliminating the word "circle," and let the group decide how to solve the problem.

OTHER IDEAS:

•If you play the game where every player has their own balloon, Karl suggests that you might want them to take the balloon with them and have them take care of the balloon for a while. Have participants bring their balloon to class each day for a week (no leaving it at school), checking in on who has their balloon and what such a responsibility had been like. (Remember sex-ed class when you had to take care of an uncooked egg for a few weeks?!)

BALLOON BASH—
Karl Rohnke

POSSIBLE OBJECTIVES: Problem Solving, Verbal Communication, Helping, Attention to Task, Listening, Consensus Building...

NEEDS: This activity requires some sort of noise maker (not too loud) like a bell or buzzer, a stop watch, and a bunch of balloons - at least two per student so you can adjust the challenge level if you want. (Yes, I know you may not have balloons in your room, but this is worth the extra trip.)

PROCEDURE: Clear the center of the room (obviously, I like open spaces – hey, exercise stimulates the brain!). Give each student a balloon to blow up nice and big and tie off – you may need to help with this one. I also like to do some pre-balloon work and have some blown up before the activity to help speed up the down time. I just lay them around the room for atmosphere (and distraction, you're right) and more to work on!

Okay, everyone has an expanded balloon with the end securely fastened, right? When you say "go," students should tap their balloons in the air. The objective is to keep all the balloons in the air as long as possible. One rule: You may not hit the same balloon more than one time in a row. The idea here is that you just can't keep hitting the same balloon over and over. You are allowed to hit a balloon again after you have hit a different balloon.

Choose a goal for the activity. For example, let's say ten touches. Each time a balloon hits the ground, ring the bell (or use another noise maker). You don't necessarily have to be the bell ringer or time keeper during this activity. You can assign a couple of students to the tasks. This gives you more to talk about. When the students hear this bell, they can do one of two things: 1) leave the fallen laytex on the ground, or 2) pick it up and tap it back into the flurry. If they pick the balloon up to add it back to the action, then no other penalty is assessed. However, if the balloon stays on the ground longer than three seconds, another bell is sounded. At ten bells, stop the time and action, and let the balloons fall where they may. (I think there are some metaphors in there?)

OBSERVATIONS/QUESTIONS:
- How was our time? Good? Bad? What are we comparing it to?
- Was there any leadership?
- Would anyone like to make any observations on the action? What was helpful? What was not?
- Do you think we can do better?
- What would be a good time to shoot for?
- What should we do differently to get a better time?

(OTHERS)

•Who gives ideas? Who doesn't? Why?
•What ideas are we going to implement?
•
•

After some of this brainstorming, give the activity another go. See what happens.

MORE OBSERVATIONS/QUESTIONS:
•How did we do?
•Were we able to implement our ideas? Why? Why not?
•Share some observations about the second round?
•What was helpful? What was not?
•What role did you take in the activity? Did we all have the same one? What is the significance of taking different roles during an activity? Is it necessary?
•What roles do we have in the classroom? In the school? At home?
•How are these roles different, and why do you think they are different? Do you think they are fair?
•What role did the instructor take during the activity? Is this common?
•How could we be more successful? Does anyone have any new ideas, or the same ideas?
•What goal do we shoot for in the next round?
•
•

(OTHERS)

If you have the time, make another attempt. If you can end with success, make sure you discuss the skills that made it successful. If you don't reach the goal, talk about why and what might be done to be more successful. Relate as much as you can to the classroom as well.

VARIATIONS:
•Add more balloons. How many can they keep up before one falls to the floor?

OTHER IDEAS:

·The most adventurous idea that I know for releasing the atmosphere in the balloons comes from Karl Rohnke. It's called "Fire in the Hole." (You might want to do this where loud noises will not be a distraction to others in the area.) Put a balloon between two people, right about the belly button area, wrap arms around each other for the BIG HUG. Don't forget to yell "FIRE IN THE HOLE!" before you squeeze. (I like to walk around with a paper clip opened up to help pop the stubborn balloons.)

OBJECTABLES —
Karl Rohnke

POSSIBLE OBJECTIVES: Problem Solving, Verbal Communication, Persistence, Attention to Task, Accepting Failure, Accepting Limitations, Accepting Diversity...

NEEDS: Two soft, throwable objects, no larger than a softball, for each person and an area for a large circle (or whatever the group forms). Tennis balls work well, so do crumpled up paper wads.

PROCEDURE: Start the group in a large circle. Each player's objective will be to toss one object to (not at) another player in the group. Everyone in the class will toss <u>at the same time</u>. Players can only receive a throw from someone they are not throwing to. Also, any one player may only possess one object at a time. How many throws can your group achieve, in a row, without dropping an object? (You can set up the classroom formation yourself or let the students figure out the best formation to use. The most challenging formation I have found is a circle of desks.)

Seem simple enough? After giving directions, this is a great one to sit back and watch. I have seen large groups fragment into smaller groups. This is fine, but make sure the rules are being followed. If they are successful with the smaller groups, ask them to try the activity again in a large group to see what happens.

I have found that walking around the classroom as they are playing helps keep individuals on track. It also gives them opportunities to ask questions, and of course you will encourage them to ask others in the class for the help they need.

OBSERVATIONS/QUESTIONS:
- What roles did students take?
- Who took leadership roles?
- Were ideas being heard?
- Which individuals were initially reactive to the activity?
- What forms of reaction were there?
- How did the group communicate with each other?
- What made the activity challenging?
- Was there anything you could do to eliminate the problems your group encountered?
- What was the advantage of splitting into smaller groups (if it happened)?
- How successful were you in small or large groups?
- How does small group work help us in this classroom?

(OTHERS)
-
-

VARIATIONS:
- Start out with two objects each.
- Try some people with two objects and others with one - it's a blast.
- If you have enough bouncable objects, try a bounce-and-catch progression.

OTHER IDEAS:

OVER THE TOP ─

POSSIBLE OBJECTIVES: Problem Solving, Compromising, Decision Making, Cooperation, Accepting Consequences...

NEEDS: All you'll need for this one is a motivating device (MD). My favorite is CHOCOLATE. However, your class might prefer something else. It should be something small that can be counted out quickly, e.g., Skittles®, M & Ms®, Reeses Pieces®, Jelly Bellies®. It doesn't have to be edible – marbles or pennies work fine too. If you can relate the MD to something you're working on in class, then all the better.

PROCEDURE: There are a few ways to set this up, but the bottom line (first) is that pairs of players will be arm wrestling each other for one minute. You can tell them this concept before or after you put them in pairs – interesting reactions in both cases. Match up students using one of the following options that will best suit the needs/issues you want to tackle.

1. Boys against boys. Girls against girls. What are the issues here?
2. Players of the same size. Does size determine success?
3. Players based on "assumed" strength. What assumptions do we make?
4. (My personal favorite.) Girls against boys? Gender issues?

NOTE: A little warning here. This activity could suggest that the winners are the "bad guys or girls." Be sure to process away from this issue and focus on the point of the exercise.

Here's how this works. After you pair up players, tell them they will be arm wrestling each other for one minute (if you haven't done so already). Notice the reactions. Every time a player touches their partner's hand to the surface, they win an MD for the class. (The total number of MDs will be shared evenly with everyone in the class.) Each time there is a touch, the pairs must go back to the "over the top" position – hands perpendicular to the floor – before another touch can be made. Players should keep track of how many times they touch their partner's hand to the surface.

I like to spread the kids out around on the floor. If they sit at a desk, the students tend to hold onto the desk for leverage - but this might be okay if you want to discuss advantages.

SAFETY NOTE: Make sure the motion of the arm pull is toward the body and not across from side-to-side. Side-to-side can cause injury to the shoulder. When they set up to wrestle, they should put their elbow on the surface. Then have them put their hand in the air so they can see their own palm (not the thumb side of the hand). Have them overlap palms with their partner. With this set up, the arm pulls will be toward the puller's face. In this position, if a player is getting her arm pulled, it will straighten out away from her and not twist the shoulder as in the side-to-side wrestling.

Set your time for 60 seconds and give them the go! Notice reactions and behaviors. After 60 seconds have them stop. Go around the room and ask each person how many MDs they were able to gain for their class. Emphasize that this is neither good or bad, it just is (one of my favorite discussion topics). Be sure to protect the emotional safety of all players. Do not allow put-downs of any kind. What is the total number of MDs so far? Throw in a few questions to discuss (still more to come).

OBSERVATIONS/QUESTIONS:
- What was your reaction when you found out you had to arm wrestle your partner?
- What are some of the assumptions you made? Winner? Loser? Competition?
- How did the assumptions turn out?
- Did I tell you this was a competitive activity?
- Did any of the pairs have a strategy to gain more MDs? What was it?
- Who won the MDs?
-
-

(OTHERS)

Now the punchline. After observing the action, I will ask the most successful arm wrestler, who is also often the strongest, to come up and wrestle with me. (Lots of OOOOs and AHHHs here). I communicate to this person that I would like to work together (cooperate) to get as many MDs as we can for our class. I agree not to resist. I ask him to agree not to resist. If there is no resistance on either part, we should be able to move back and forth quite a few times in one minute. I ask a student to time us and one to start and stop us. Go! Stop! How many did we get?

MORE OBSERVATIONS/QUESTIONS:
- What did we assume about the first round of this activity?
- What was different about the way I arm wrestled with my partner?
- How could our class benefit from cooperation?
- When do you think cooperation will be useful in our class?
- Can we name some characteristics of cooperation?
- Who has a thought about competition? Good? Bad?
- How can competition help our class?
- Let's split up our winnings and enjoy them!
-
-

(OTHERS)

91

VARIATIONS:

OTHER IDEAS:

A WHAT? ___
Karl Rohnke

POSSIBLE OBJECTIVES: Attention to Task, Listening, Verbal Communication...

NEEDS: Grab four objects from the room. Objects that will not break when dropped and will not break anything if dropped (e.g., book, pencil, box of tissue, piece of paper).

PROCEDURE: This one's a bit hard to grasp by reading, but we had to add it because it's just plain fun!! If this one doesn't sink in, call us for a workshop. We love to play!

Have the group sit in a circle. Pick two students sitting side-by-side to be the starting points. For this description we will designate these two as the driver (left person) and the passenger (right person). Hand the passenger the pencil (or whatever object you're using). The passenger turns to the person on her right (player #1), holds up the pencil and says, "This is a Basketball!" (Basketball is not a misprint - just part of the fun.) Player #1 takes the pencil, with a bit of surprise and asks the passenger, "A What?" The passenger states again, "A Basketball!" Player #1 holds up the pencil to the person on his right (player #2) and says, "This is a Basketball!" Player #2 takes the pencil and with some surprise asks player #1, "A What?" Player #1 turns to the passenger and asks, "A What?" The passenger replies, "A Basketball." Player #1 turns back to player #2 and confirms, "A Basketball." This process continues down the line. "A What" is always passed all the way back around to the passenger and the name of the object is passed all the way back to the player holding the object.

Once the players understand the action to the right, stop and show them the next pattern to the left. Hand the book (or whatever object you are using) to the driver. Practice the same action to the left. "A What" is always passed back to the driver. The name of the object is always passed back to the person holding the object. Practice through the first few players so everyone gets the idea.

Everyone gets the concept, right? Now, what I like to do to make things interesting is change the driver and passenger. Put the book and pencil away. Pick two new starters - I usually go with the two directly across from the original starters (these players haven't had the chance to do anything yet). Hand out the piece of paper to the new driver and the tissue to the passenger. Ready? Go! They saw how to do it! This game starts to really get fun when the objects cross each other.

OBSERVATIONS/QUESTIONS:

- Was everyone able to grasp the process of the game?
- What was difficult about the game?
- Did anyone make a mistake during the game? What did you do about it? How did the other players in the group react?
- What would be the best way to treat people when they make a mistake?
- When did the game get really difficult?
- How do you handle confusion?
- Were you able to concentrate during the process?
- What was the volume level of the activity? Why do you think this was happening?
- What can happen when people talk at the same time?
- Does anyone know what the "rule of loud" means?
- Do you think the "rule of loud" is necessary? How do we prevent it?
- What did you learn from A WHAT?
-
-

(OTHERS)

VARIATIONS:

- Keep both sets of starters and start all four objects at the same time. Chaos reigns a bit quicker in this one.

OTHER IDEAS:

QUICK NUMBERS —
Frank Aycox

POSSIBLE OBJECTIVES: Attention to Task, Accepting/Supporting Failure, Willingness, Consensus Building...

NEEDS: A separate chair for each player works the best, but the all-in-one desk will work out fine also. Circle the chairs, facing them toward the center. (Come to think of it, <u>sitting</u> in a big circle would work too.)

PROCEDURE: Players are numbered around the circle, skipping the number four. There will not be a number four player (at least there is not supposed to be). The number one player always starts the game by calling the number of another player (this might be a good opportunity to give this initial leadership role - #1 - to someone in the class who may not be considered a leader). The player whose number is called must immediately call the number of another player, and so on. A player makes a mistake if he either hesitates, stutters or mispronounces, laughs, calls out his own number, answers out of turn, or calls the number four! (Remember, there is no number four.)

> **NOTE:** At different points in the game, someone will need to be the "judge(s)." As the teacher, you will need to decide if the group is ready to take on this role or if you will assume this role yourself. Letting the group do this will surely empower them toward community building. However, you may need to discuss to what degree the mistakes will be accepted and appropriate ways to "judge" and how we can react to being judged. All good social skills to prepare for if the time is available.

So, on with the game. At the point of the mistake the game stops. The erring player gets demoted to the last seat as the players behind him move up one chair.

> **Phase One:** Continue the game - player number one starts - with all players keeping their original numbers.
>
> -or-
>
> **Phase Two:** The numbers belong to the chairs, so when players move they must assume their new number based on where they are sitting. After all players learn their new numbers, the player in chair number one restarts the next round.
>
> -or-
>
> **Phase Three:** The numbers belong to the chairs, so when players move they must assume their new number based on where they are sitting. Number one starts the game once all players are seated in their new positions – there is no discussion of new numbers.

The three phases of the game are presented as a progression. You can choose to go in order or play any of the phases depending on the challenge level your group is ready for. You can also choose to play more than one phase in one sitting or spread them out over a period of time as your class matures.

OBSERVATIONS/QUESTIONS:

- What do you think was the point of the game? What is important about each point? How can these points help our class?
- What was it like being number one?
- How important is it to be number one?
- Who wanted to get to the number one seat?
- Was anyone's number not called? How did you feel about that?
- Did you experience success even if your number wasn't called? Why? Is this a good way to be successful? How can you take control over your own success?
- What were some personal goals you had during the game?
- What did you feel like when you made a mistake?
- How did the group react to the mistakes made?
- What are some ways we can show support for our class when mistakes are made?
- Why is support important in our classroom?
- Share some feelings you were having during the game? At what other times during our class do you have these feelings? What do you do about these feelings?
-
-

(OTHERS)

VARIATIONS:

- Mr. Aycox states that, "The objective of the game is for every player to strive to become number one by not making any errors." You could present this goal to the class if you want to observe the competitive nature of your students.
- What if you made all the choices for them? Say you had a variety of numbered cards - one for each player. You would hold up one number at a time for the players to call. Say you hold up a number five, the number one player calls number five. When five is called, you change number cards to a number ten. The number five player has to call number ten, and so on. What does this do? As teachers, do we tend to make too many choices for our class? How do our students react? What is the energy level of this variation compared to one of the phases above?

OTHER IDEAS:

TOUCH —
Frank Aycox

POSSIBLE OBJECTIVES: Trust, Sharing, Listening, Responsibility, Decision Making, Problem Solving...

NEEDS: No additional props needed other than all the contents of a normal classroom.

PROCEDURE: You will need a caller for this one. Depending on the age of your group you could be the first caller or let the students take turns being the caller. I tend to pick leaders one at a time. This gives me a chance to give each student name recognition and attention. If the energy is good, I will go through all the students in the class. If the energy goes down, I will end the activity early and return to it another time.

The designated leader names something in the room and the players touch it. Players can touch as much as they want, using one finger or two hands. Players are free to move about the room to accomplish the task. When everyone in the room is performing the touch (and everyone in the room has stopped moving), a new leader chooses another item in the room. Simple!?

I'll bet most of you have reacted the same way I did when I first read this. Let me continue with Mr. Aycox's elaboration.

"I have put this ultra-simple game to heavy duty use for many years. As a closure activity it can bring a group together at the end of a social play session beautifully.

With older students, sexual joking usually occurs during the game...but I never go past the comfort level. As a matter of fact, here is the usual rundown of things I suggest to touch (you be the judge): a color, leather, metal jewelry, a fabric, a person (tallest, smallest, leader, etc.), a shoulder or two, a knee, a smile, hands, etc. What the leader must do is start out in a nonthreatening manner and move up to things that are more intimate. With younger students, colors and textures can be educational while older students focus more on the need to be touched.

I frequently end TOUCH by having all the players touch all the hands in a big circle and doing a rousing team cheer with hands raised high!"

This is a wonderful activity, for all ages, to promote discussions about boundaries - both personal and classroom. I'm sure you can picture some of the differences you will encounter with the age level of your class. If you do this activity at different times of the year, you will also get different actions and reactions. Always remember - the objective of this book - that appropriate social interaction and behavior is the goal.

97

OBSERVATIONS/QUESTIONS:

·What was your initial reaction to the activity? Why do you think we have those reactions?
·What sort of boundaries do we need to establish in our classroom?
·Why are boundaries important? Classroom? Personal?
·Did anyone feel that we violated any boundaries during the game?
·Who would like to share any of their personal boundaries with the class?
·Was anyone uncomfortable with any of the touches?
·Did anyone choose not to touch?
·How did you decide what to have your classmates touch?
·Which students took more risks than others? Why?
·
·

(OTHERS)

VARIATIONS:

·To build in a little more teamwork, have the students work together in pairs. They should be attached in some way - lock elbows, hold hands, train line. Being attached will force a bit more communication between classmates. You could also call a "change" every once in a while to mix up partners.

OTHER IDEAS:

SENSORY MASTERPIECE —

POSSIBLE OBJECTIVES: Non-Verbal Communication, Attention to Task, Accepting Limitations...

NEEDS: Included in this activity are several pictures - a star, a house, and the silhouette of a dog. You will need a copy of the star and house for each pair of students in your class and one silhouette of the dog for every group of six students. You will also need some blank paper and some fun-colored crayons or water-based markers. (If you have a large dry-erase board or chalkboard you can use this also.)

PROCEDURE: Pair up your students. (Groups of three will be hard to manage, and you will not be able to play. So, play on an even-student day or borrow another child. Maybe the principal is free?). Ask each pair to choose who will be the first drawer and who will be the first artist - they will switch roles after the first round. Have the drawers sit at their desk with a blank sheet of paper and a colorful writing implement. All the artists need to come to you for the secret picture - let's say the star. The artists do not want their drawing partners to see the star - just yet. With picture in hand, the artists return to their drawing partners and stand behind them.

Now for some action. The objective is for the artists, using their magic pencil (that being their pointer/index finger), to outline a rendition of the secret picture on the backs of their partners. The drawing partners do their best to sense the rendition and draw it on their paper. Give all the pairs one or two minutes to do this.

During this interaction the drawers may talk to the artists, but at no time can the artists talk to the drawers. Comments tend to be limited to: slow down, could you repeat that part, start over. Questions requiring a verbal response are to be avoided for obvious reasons.

When the time is up, the secret picture can be revealed. Allow a little time for reactions before you have partners switch roles. Have the new artists come up for their secret picture – the house. Give the pairs one minute to attempt the transfer. Compare pictures, then take a little process break.

OBSERVATIONS/QUESTIONS:
- What was that activity like for the drawers? Artists?
- What was the most difficult part of the activity?
- What sort of communication was taking place?
- Did any of the drawers communicate with their partners?
- Did the artists use all the time they were given?
- Where was the focus of your attention? Were there any distractions?

•How did your drawings match up? Were they identical? Why not?
•What types of communication can we use? What can be said about the different types of communication?

(OTHERS)
•
•

If you have the time, and their attention, to take this a step further, put students together in groups of six (I usually just put three pairs together). If you have a dry-erase board or chalkboard, line the students in front of the board - first person in line (the drawer-to-be) is facing the board, the rest of the group is lined up behind the first person. If you need to use paper and crayons, then just have the students sit in their desks in rows - this works just as well.

I'm sure you can imagine (so can they at this point) what is going to happen. The last person in line will need to get the secret picture from you - the silhouette of the dog. Give them 60 seconds to transfer this picture up the line – each student in the group should be drawing at the same time. When the time is up, the artist goes to the drawer to share the secret picture.

MORE OBSERVATIONS/QUESTIONS:

•How was this version?
•What was the difference between the two versions?
•Was everyone able to concentrate on the drawing? What made it difficult to concentrate?
•What can this activity tell us about communication?
•Are there any situations in a school setting that are similar to this?
•What are some skills we are using in class to communicate effectively?
•What are some skills we might want to use in our class for more effective communication?

(OTHERS)
•
•

VARIATIONS:

•Instead of outlining the picture on the partner's back, just stand behind them and give verbal directions about the picture - no correcting the drawer!

OTHER IDEAS:

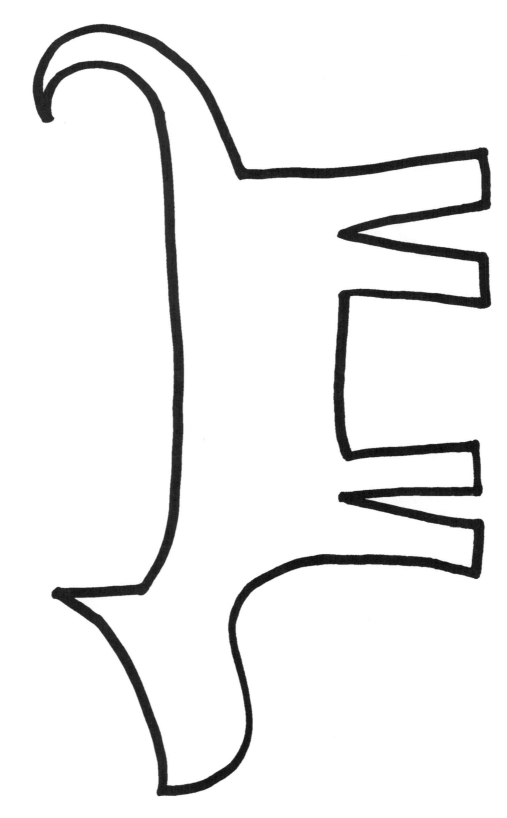

THE MIXING GAME—

Kathy Hellenbrand

POSSIBLE OBJECTIVES: Listening, Inclusion, Decision Making, Accepting Consequences, Accepting Others...

NEEDS: No props are needed for this one, just a little work. It would be ideal to clear as much of the middle of the room as you can.

PROCEDURE: This activity deals directly with getting partners and being able to work with anyone in the group. Ask all the students to stand in the open area of the classroom and give them the word of the day. (Make up something fun. I like to use a word that rhymes with a lot of things so I can fake them out. If the word of the day is PICKLE, I can fake them out with, tickle, sickle, fickle, nickel, trickle and the like. A good way to work on listening skills.) Tell them that when you say the word of the day, each student will have to the count of five to get a partner and hold his or her hand up in the air. If a player does not get a partner in that amount of time, they should join you to help count for the next rounds. Continue calling out the word of the day followed by the countdown until only a few partners are left.

So, you ask about countdown speed. The older the group is, the faster I tend to count. But that's just me. Kathy's advice is to keep the game fast-paced. As the students focus on speed, they tend to forget about being choosy. It's an interesting concept to watch. The slower you go, the more people you catch without a partner. When there is time to think, judgement seems to slow the decision process down. What else slows down in the classroom when there is time to judge?

Try a few rounds of THE MIXING GAME to see if any of the dynamics change. Keep an eye out for the students who are always the first ones out. This might indicate a lack of social skills – something you can work together on so they can feel more comfortable with their classmates.

OBSERVATIONS/QUESTIONS:
- Was the game easy or hard for you? What made it this way?
- Who did you partner with the first round? Why?
- What was it like to be without a partner? What did you do?
- Did anyone feel left out? What can you do about this feeling? Would you like to do something new in the future? What are some ways we can get more involved with others?
- Did anyone choose not to find a partner? Why?
- What does it mean to be pro-active? How can we benefit from this?

·What motivated you to find a partner? Why did you try?
·Did anyone partner with someone they really didn't know very well? How did this feel?
·Why might it be important to be able to work with everyone in the class?
·Is it okay to work with people that are not your friends?
·What might be some bad things about leaving people out of the group/clique?
·What are some positive things about working with new people?

(OTHERS)
·
·

VARIATIONS:

·This variation has a nice twist of honesty to it. With every change, each student has to find a person they have not paired up with in the previous round. In other words, you can't match up with the same player more than once. Add some questions about honesty, integrity, and reputation.

OTHER IDEAS:

·For a non-elimination partner activity, try FRONT-TO-FRONT.

FRONT-TO-FRONT—
Adapted from Frank Aycox & Frank Harris

POSSIBLE OBJECTIVES: Trust, Problem Solving, Listening, Cooperation, Helping, Support, Accepting Limitations, Non-Verbal Communication...

NEEDS: Nothing needed except a nice open area in the middle of your room.

PROCEDURE: Partner up students in the middle of the room. A group of three works fine if there is an extra player. To start with, you will be giving the group one of three commands: "Front-to-Front," "Back-to-Back," or "Mix." When you say "Front-to-Front," the pairs face each other. I like to emphasize the use of eye contact while the students are "Front-to-Front" (a little discussion about eye contact might not be bad prior to this activity). When you say "Back-to-Back," students turn away from their partner and stand back-to-back (you got that I'm sure). Eye contact is also very helpful during the back-to-back part as well. If students can establish eye contact with other players, they might be more ready for a mix. When you call "Mix," players have to match up with a different partner and stand together, shoulder-to-shoulder, ready for the next call.

Go through about nine or ten calls, then add some more challenge. When you call "Challenge," each small group will attempt to sit on the floor, then stand back up again, attached to each other at all times. If the small groups are facing each other as they attempt to sit and stand, every hand has to hold another hand (not a player's own hand) and every foot has to touch another foot (not a player's own foot). If they are back-to-back, then each back must be touching another back when going down and coming back up again – do not lock arms together at the elbows!

Now as you might have noticed, I have been using the words "small group." After you do a couple of challenges in pairs, call out "Groups of three Mix." As you might guess, this means that three people must stand shoulder-to-shoulder-to-shoulder and prepare for the next call. When you call "Challenge," groups of three have to follow the same guidelines as pairs: If the small groups are facing each other as they attempt to sit and stand, every hand has to hold another hand (not a player's own hand), and every foot has to touch another foot (not a player's own foot). If the small groups are back-to-back, then each back must be touching another back when going down and coming back up again – do not lock arms together at the elbows! What if you call for groups of four, five, six or seven to mix? The Challenge gets a bit more challenging.

SAFETY NOTE: There is a potential for falling over during this activity. So for some obvious reasons I do not attempt the activity until I think the group is ready for it. Have a safety talk with the students and make sure they understand the

107

importance of taking care of each other and themselves. Ask them to stay away from desks or any other object in the room they might fall on. (Space in your classroom might be a factor here. If you could head outside in a grassy area for this one, you could get rid of a great number of those safety issues - plus, wouldn't it be nice to get outside for some fresh air!)

OBSERVATIONS/QUESTIONS:
- What was it like to have eye contact with another person? Was it hard for you to do? Why do you think this is a hard thing to achieve?
- Were you able to find a small group every time? Why?
- Did you look for someone to move to or did you wait for someone to come to you?
- What was the most challenging part of the activity - before the challenges?
- Did you tend to get together with different students at each mix or gather with the same students? What was your reason for doing this?
- What would be an advantage to working with many different people?
- What were the challenges like for you?
- Were you careful during the challenges or reckless? Why?
- Why do you think some of us might choose to be reckless? How does this affect our class?
- Rate your success at the challenges.
- Were the small groups or larger groups easier? Why?
- Do you think we could figure out how to achieve a stand with the entire group? (see variation below)

(OTHERS)
-
-

VARIATIONS:
- If you have the time to attempt a finale, try "Everybody Up." From a sitting position, every player must be in contact with everyone else. This means that if (emphasis on IF) you ran a low-voltage current through the group, everyone would get a little jolt - I did say low voltage! Students must all start on their seats without crossing their feet. Go.

OTHER IDEAS:

CLIQUES ▬

1996 Activity Colloquium in Tulsa, OK., Sam Sikes & Michael Gass

POSSIBLE OBJECTIVES: Problem Solving, Sharing, Inclusion, Helping, Trust, Verbal Communication...

NEEDS: All you will need for this one is a few rolls of masking tape. It would be ideal if every group of three could have their own roll, but groups can share (a nice social skill).

PROCEDURE: Clear the center of the room as much as you can. Ask your students to get into groups of four. More than likely they will get together with the students they are comfortable with – cliques of a sort. Using masking tape, ask each group to create a box on the floor big enough for all their group members to fit into with just enough extra room for a small trash can. (No, you don't need a trash can. I just wanted to state in simple terms not to make the squares too big.)

Ask all the players to put both feet inside their square. Have them introduce themselves to everyone in the square (another good social skill). Then use one of the questions provided to initiate some verbal communication within the clique. Ask for their attention and tell them that when you say "change," each player must move to another square. When all players have both feet inside a new square, ask them to introduce themselves to all the people in the square. Then ask another intriguing, interactive question.

Do this mingle/change for a few rounds. Observe the interaction. Then before each change, start taking away one square at a time by pulling up the tape from the floor. Obviously there will start to be more people in each square. Don't forget the introductions and intriguing questions.

As the rounds progress, you will want to be very safety conscious. Students will start to "hang" off each other. I do not let the students piggy-back (hard to have both feet in a square this way, too). Try to suggest some helpful ways to stay in the squares. I also tend to remove the squares near desks and other objects that students might fall onto. Or, you might use the desks to your advantage so students can hold themselves up – using classroom resources. When it comes down to a couple of squares, make sure these are in the middle of the room. Depending on the size of your group, you might not want to go down to one square. The key is to create a challenge for them. They will have to find a way for all the students to have both feet in a square. Can you break out of the "clique."

Did you figure it out? The most common solution is sitting down on the floor and resting their feet inside the box instead of struggling for balance while trying to stand.

This is a challenging problem to solve. If I do this activity early on, my objectives are more toward verbal communication, sharing, and helping - with maybe a little problem-solving. I will end the activity when the groups have had a little challenge and are still able to fit in the squares with some physical help – getting down to maybe three or four squares. I use the "get aquainted" questions and end with success. Later in the year, I may do this again, building on past experience. I'll use some of the more personal questions and try to get down to one square. All this will depend on the maturity of your group and how far you want to take them.

POSSIBLE QUESTIONS

What's your favorite color?
How many brothers and sisters do you have?
What did you have for breakfast?
What has been your favorite movie so far?
What is your favorite subject in school?
What is your favorite sport to watch or play?
Would you rather be rich, famous or happy?
What mood are you in right now?
What part of the day do you like the most?
Name one food you could eat every meal?
What would you like to get for your next birthday?
If you were a teacher, what subject could you teach the best right now?
How many feet are in your square? (Did you count the square feet of the square?)
If you had one wish, what would you wish for?

OBSERVATIONS/QUESTIONS:

- Think about the first group you were in. Why did you choose this group?
- What was comfortable about this group?
- When you changed squares, did you stay with the same group or get in a square with some other students? Why?
- Did you ever feel uncomfortable with anyone in a square? Why/why not?
- How do we get to know someone we don't know? What is good about this? What might be hard about this?
- Did you talk to someone that you don't normally talk to? What was this like?
- Did you learn something new about someone in the class? Can you share it?
- What was the reaction to the squares being pulled up?
- What tends to happen to you when things get more difficult? Is this reaction something you want to change? How could you change it?
- What did you do, as a group, to adapt to the change? Was it safe? Unsafe?
- What can we do in this class to help each other through the difficult moments?
- What was the final challenge like? Did you succeed?
- How do you feel when you succeed? How do you feel when you fail?
- Will there be times in class when you will succeed or fail? How will you respond?
- So, how many feet did you get into one square?
-
-

(OTHERS)

110

VARIATIONS:

•Every time the students change, add a different locomotor movement - hopping, skipping, sliding (great on carpet for shocking introductions), backwards (careful)...

OTHER IDEAS:

COMMUNITY BOX —
Sam Sikes

POSSIBLE OBJECTIVES: Cooperation, Decision Making, Consensus Building, Inclusion, Verbal Communication, Sharing, Problem Solving...

NEEDS: One roll of masking tape and 12 sheets of 8 1/2" x 11" paper.

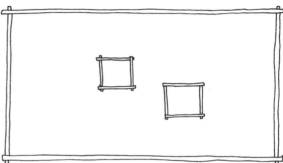

PROCEDURE: Set up the playing area as diagrammed, using masking tape for the boundaries. The outside boundaries (make this as big as your room allows) are in a rectangle shape, but a square could be used. (A rectangle shape will bring up issues of fairness if this is a program goal.) The squares in the middle are 2' x 2'.

This activity can be done with small or large groups. Split the group into four smaller teams (but they are still one group), each team standing outside one side of the boundary area. Give each team three sheets of paper. The objective is for the teams on opposite sides to exchange places, as quickly as possible, without stepping on the floor or ground when inside the rectangle. Here are the other parameters:

1) The boundary area and squares inside may not be moved in any way.
2) No more than three feet may be on any sheet of paper at one time.
3) The squares inside the area are safe zones (you can step inside them) but once utilized, they must <u>always</u> be occupied by two people within a reasonable amount of time (someone must be stepping into it as someone is stepping out), or the square is lost.
4) Loss of human contact with a sheet of paper results in the loss of the paper. Any momentary loss of contact, take away the resource.
5) You may not enter the rectangle from any other side than the one you started on.
6) You may only exit through the opposite side from where you started.
7) You may not "scoot" or "ski" across the rectangle.
8) No jumping - an unsafe process.
9) Paper cannot be thrown - it violates rule #4.
10) If anyone fails to follow any of the parameters, they must go back to their starting side.

With all that said and done, what is the concept? The hidden agenda has to deal with sharing resources. If all the teams would share their resources and create a diagonal line - as a group, from one corner across to another (dividing the rectangle into two triangles) - switching sides would go much faster. In most cases that I have seen, it has been "all teams for themselves." After losing resources, some teams will figure out the sharing concept, or at least help another team. In any case, it has always been very interesting to watch.

The group as a whole may get to a point where they can no longer move. What are the options? If they ask to start again, they must tell you one thing they will do differently on the next try.

OBSERVATIONS/QUESTIONS:

- What sort of planning took place?..by small group?..by large group?
- Was there any sharing of ideas? Any copying?
- Is copying good?..bad?..cheating?
- What was the reaction over losing a resource? Who was blamed?
- How did groups "regroup" after losing resources?
- Were you working together?
- Who gave you the rules of the game? Did you accept them? Did you ever try to challenge them? Did you ever ask to change any of the rules? How would changing the rules affect the activity?
- Is there a way you could all work together to be more successful - if success was measured by a better time?
- What are some keys to becoming more successful?
- What is the overall reaction to the processes you were involved in?

(OTHERS)
-
-

VARIATIONS: As suggested in the original text, there are a few ways to force the sharing idea a little faster if desired.

- Change rule #2 above to read: "No more than two feet may be on any square at one time."
- Add this as rule #11 - You may not contact or use the same square twice in succession. Once you lose contact with a square or have used the square, someone else must be in contact with it *before* you may come into contact with it again. Define "use a square" - it means to make progress toward your goal.
- Use only eight total squares. Give two squares to each side.

OTHER IDEAS:

- Make a sheet of rules for the group, and hand it to them. Make them the experts.

GOTCHA LINES —
Craig Dobkin via Karl Rohnke via the Australia/Collard Connection

POSSIBLE OBJECTIVES: Listening, Attention to Task, Consensus Building, Decision Making...

NEEDS: There are no props for this challenge. Hearing ability is needed.

PROCEDURE: First, let's go over the basic game of GOTCHA LINES as we know it. Have the group stand or sit (Karl even suggests squatting - this would add an interesting physical component to the task) in a large circle. (Yes, you will probably need to move the desks out of the way again.) If you missed that, the group needs to be in a big circle. Ask each person to face the center of the circle, place their left hand out in front of them, elbow bent at 90 degrees, with their palm up. Now, point the index finger (the pointer finger as my young students know it) of their right hand down toward the left palm of the person standing to their right. On "go," players attempt to touch the left palm of the person to their right with their index finger without being caught. The one proviso is that the left arm and hand must stay in the general 90 degree mode - you can't reach up to grab a finger, only close the hand.

Give the basic "Gotcha" a few tries before moving into "Gotcha Lines."

Now, let's add to the fun. Craig likes to add some creative story telling and listening skills. First, the group has to agree on a secret word that will replace the word "go" in the standard game. For our example let's use "unbelievable." Then choose someone to start out a story. This will be an add-on story, Someone starts, then the next person adds on, the next person adds on, and so on. During any time in the story when the word "unbelievable" is used, all the right pointer fingers should attempt the left palm touch and left hands should try to catch the finger.

Craig also suggests that you can use this game to review for upcoming tests or share facts from lessons. Any time you can use an activity to support a lesson, the better chance for learning moments. Just use a secret word related to the lesson.

I have provided a couple of sample story lines in case you want to use some progression with this activity. Once the students understand how it works, they might have an easier time with their own stories.

OBSERVATIONS/QUESTIONS:
- What did you think of the activity? Was it difficult?
- Were you able to follow the directions?
- Were you able to catch any pointers?

•How many things were you doing at any one time? At which one were you best?
 Why?
•How many things do you think you are capable of doing at one time?
•How many things are you capable of doing well at one time?
•Did anyone have any fun?
•
•

(OTHERS)

VARIATIONS:

•Read something from Shakespeare – there are lots of secret words to choose
from!
•You could break this activity down even further if you wanted to emphasize the
"one-thing-at-a-time" concept. Start out with pairs. Face each other. One person
does the palm, the other the finger (not that finger). Say "go." What is the catch
to miss ratio - it will be better than the large circle version. From here go to
Gotcha, then Gotcha Lines. (This could be a good math activity on ratio. Just plot
catches.)

STORY LINE IDEAS:

NATHAN (secret word is unbelievable)
Nathan was an underachiever, but a very determined young lad. It was not too
unbelievable to imagine that under Nathan's cool exterior was unbridled energy.
"Unbelievable," he would shout over his math book. "Unbelievable," he would cry
over his spelling book. "Unnecessary," he would proclaim over his English assign-
ments. "I'm uncharacteristically excellent in the English language. I don't lack any
understanding." So, as unbelievable as it may seem, Nathan scored under all his
classmates and still kept his unbelievable happy manner. The End. Unbelievable
story, isn't it? (Really the end.)

ANN (secret word is outstanding)
Ann goes to Art class every day, and she is an outstanding artist. According to her
teacher, she is outgoing and creative. Ideas just pop out of her head flowing
outward as if her mind were a fountain. Just like the beautiful fountain outside
the Van Gogh School of Art.

"Your work is outstanding, Ann!" says her teacher.

"What an outstanding drawing!" her friends exclaim.

115

But Ann is very down-to-earth and does not let all the compliments go to her head. At one point she felt like an outcast because of her different way of doing things. What she really wants is to be part of her group.

"Someday I will be an outstanding artist," she says to herself. "But no matter what the outcome, in the meantime I must strive to be an outstanding human being." Little does she know that she already is!

OTHER IDEAS:

CENTERPIECE —
Experiential Community

POSSIBLE OBJECTIVES: Problem Solving, Decision Making, Cooperation, Attention to Task...

NEEDS: You will need a stop watch and one central object for this activity, e.g., a globe (my personal favorite), a trash can, a book, a large plastic pink flamingo, a pencil, etc. (the smaller the object the greater the challenge). Yes, this object will start in the center, be the centerpiece, the central focus....you get the idea so far.

PROCEDURE: Clear the center of your room as best as you can. If you can put your desks in a circle, this would add some focus also. Have all your students stand and form a large circle in the open area. If each student could be standing in front of a desk, the desk could mark each student's starting point. Place your centerpiece on the floor in the center of the circle. You're set to go.

Ask your students to look across the circle and find someone they are going to trade places with. I will have students point at each other, e.g., if Sam is pointing to Bill, Bill should be pointing back at Sam. Make sure everyone has another person to switch with. If there is an odd number of students, then I jump in and play. (But I don't do any problem solving!)

Now for the objective. The first challenge is to switch places with your partner as fast as possible. (You might want to interject some safety rules here if you think it is necessary.) "Is everyone ready?" By asking this question you are giving the students an opportunity to ask questions that may lead to some problem solving. "Timer ready?" "Go!" "Stop!" (You can be the official starter and stopper, or ask the group to choose one of their classmates.) Take a little process break.

OBSERVATIONS/QUESTIONS:
- How did we do?
- What was the action like during the changing?
- Did anyone feel unsafe? What did you do about it?
- Did anyone have a special strategy to make it to their new spot?
- Do you think we can do better? How? Who has an idea? (Problem solving opportunity.)
-
-

(OTHERS)

Try the activity again to see if the record can be broken. Ask the group if they can come to a consensus on an idea, based on ideas given and an achievable time to finish.

This first round is usually completed in a fairly fast time - call this your "base time." For the second round, have everyone switch places as before; however, this time every player has to touch the centerpiece before proceeding to their new spot. (Warning: Please caution players about potential head-butting.) Same activity, added rule - this never happens. "Is everyone ready?" "Go!" "Stop!" "How did we do?" More processing. Problem solve with the students and then try to beat the base time.

To achieve a faster time, the group will have to "think out of the box." The box is the place we get into when we keep doing the same thing over and over, and we can't see another way to produce the same result – or better results. Problem solve with your kids. (Did you ever say that you couldn't pick up the centerpiece?)

MORE OBSERVATIONS/QUESTIONS:

- Is there any leadership in the group? Who? What kind?
- What was different about the two rounds?
- What were some of the ideas shared with the group? How were these ideas accepted? Was the reaction toward the person or the idea?
- How many ideas were you able to try? How many ideas were given?
- What is good about ideas?
- Is it better to have just a few ideas about something or a lot of ideas? Why?
- Who had an idea they didn't share? Why?
- Does anyone know what it means to "think out of the box"?
- How can we benefit from "thinking out of the box"?

(OTHERS)
-
-

VARIATIONS:

- I will use this challenge when I want to talk about honesty and accountability. (It comes from the original activity that CENTERPIECE derived from, "Don't Touch Me.") During the second round crossing, students may not touch anyone in any manner. When "stop" is called, ask if there were any touches – some honesty involved. Add one second for each touch. Even with this challenge, the group can still beat the base time.

OTHER IDEAS:

A VERY LARGE KNOT —

POSSIBLE OBJECTIVES: Problem Solving, Verbal Communication, Cooperation...

NEEDS: This is a prop-free activity. If you are working with a population that has trouble with holding hands or cannot hold hands, use something they could hold onto, e.g., rubber bands, rolled-up paper, bandannas, tissue (they cannot tear it – good added challenge), you get the idea.

PROCEDURE: Open up the center of the room so your students can form a large circle standing shoulder-to-shoulder. Ask each student to look at the person on their left and then the person on their right. Then tell the students that at the end of this activity, those two people should be on opposite sides of where they started. The person on the left will be on the right and vise versa.

With this reference in mind, ask everyone to cross arms in front of themselves and hold onto the hands of the players next to them. When everyone is attached, ask them, as a group, to untie the knot without letting go of hands. Everyone should be facing center before the hands are released. Easy?!

The quick solution is just to turn around, thus uncrossing the arms. The problem is that everyone is facing the wrong direction, away from the center of the circle. Usually there are a few students who visualize the key – everyone must go over or under the arms at a single point in the group. This causes the group to turn themselves inside out, making everyone face the center of the circle, arms uncrossed, with the two side people having switched places.

This is a simple activity that usually takes a short amount of time, but offers much to talk about.

OBSERVATIONS/QUESTIONS:
- What did you think of the activity?
- Did anyone make any assumptions about it?
- What were some of the skills you had to use to complete the task?
- What sort of leadership evolved in the group?
- How did you solve the problem?..one idea?..a combination of ideas?
- Was everyone safe during the activity?
- Did you follow the rules?
- Who makes rules? Why do you think we have rules?
- Is there a rule in this classroom that you don't understand? Why do you think it was made?
- If there was one rule you could change, what would it be?
-
-

(OTHERS)

VARIATIONS:

•If your desks are in rows, leave them that way. Form a big circle around the desks – or as many as possible. Now, try the activity. What sorts of obstacles get in the way? How can we overcome the obstacles?

OTHER IDEAS:

TOE JAM —
Craig Dobkin

POSSIBLE OBJECTIVES: Helping, Sharing, Patience, Accepting Consequences, Problem Solving...

NEEDS: You will need one roll of masking tape.

PROCEDURE: Make a masking tape square on the floor. This square should accommodate up to one quarter of your students on each side. Ask the students to split themselves into four even groups. Then ask each group to stand along a side of the square facing in, toward the center. At this point, guide the students through the following progression until you feel they have reached their challenge level.

Challenge 1: Everyone stand with both feet on the masking tape for a count of six seconds. (Sounds easy, doesn't it?!) "Want another challenge?"

Challenge 2: Walking along the masking tape, circumnavigate the square and return to your starting position. Any foot that is on the floor must be touching the tape. "Want another challenge?"

Challenge 3: Ask each student to look, and point, at the spot on the masking tape directly across from them. Then ask each student to get to that spot without stepping off the masking tape. (Most groups think they just have to walk around the square, but.... Here's where we hope to see some helping happen - if it already hasn't.) "Want another challenge?"

Challenge 4: Give each side of the square a number in clockwise order, ask students on sides 1 and 2 to switch sides and end up in the exact same order on the new side (any foot on the floor must be touching the masking tape). Ask 3 and 4 to do the same. "Want another challenge?"

Challenge 5: Have the students on sides 2 and 4, 1 and 3 change. End up in the same order on the new side. (This one is interesting, because the solution is just walking around the sides again, but many groups get stuck in the mental model of doing it like the last challenge. Fun to talk about!) "Want another challenge?"

Challenge 6: Blindfold every other student, then move around the square to end up in each student's starting position. "And another?"

Challenge 7: Blindfold all students and move around one board.

If at any time during these challenges a student touches the floor without tape contact,

121

that person has to start over from their original position, or the person next to the toucher has to start over, or the entire group starts over. Each consequence has its own issues.

SAFETY NOTE: Make sure the area around the square is free of obstacles.

OBSERVATIONS/QUESTIONS:
•What was hard about the activity you tried? What made it easier?
•What happened when someone started to fall?
•Could falls have been prevented? How?
•How did you help the group during the activity?
•Is it hard for you to ask for help? To give help? Why do you think...?
•Is it okay to ask for help?
•What did you observe during the activity?
•Who can remember what was going through your mind during the activity?
•How did you solve challenge 5? Was there another way?
•What does it mean to "think before you act?" How would this help you in the future?

(OTHERS)
•
•

VARIATIONS:
•If I have time, I like to add this introduction activity before I start the challenges. I've seen Craig Dobkin use this set up as a recognition activity. All the students stand around the square. One at a time, students step into the masking tape square, state their name and share a positive characteristic about themself. (I've found that many students have trouble stepping out from or into the group.)
•Have students attempt any of the suggested challenges non-verbally.
•For smaller groups you could use a smaller square or triangle shape. (Using a triangle makes the corner transitions a bit easier also.)

OTHER IDEAS:

CLASSROOM PARTS—
Jackie Gerstein

POSSIBLE OBJECTIVES: Trust, Cooperation, Problem Solving, Persistence, Helping, Patience, Compromising...

NEEDS: Divide your students into groups of four. If you have extras, adjust your groups accordingly based on the directions below. Each group will need one deflated balloon. The groups will be crossing the room in some manner so you should clear the middle of the room of all obstacles.

PROCEDURE: Ask each group to find their own area near one of the walls of the room. Give each group one deflated balloon and your interpretation of this sample introduction: "As a unit, you are being asked to blow up a balloon, tie it, cross the room to the opposite wall, and then break the balloon – in that order. However, you must first decide who will play what parts in your unit. Each unit will be allowed to use four legs, three hands, two eyes and one mouth. After you decide who will play what parts, only the person chosen as the mouth will be allowed to speak. You, as a unit, can only use the decided-upon body parts to blow up the balloon, tie the balloon, cross the room, and burst the balloon. Also, because all unit members are 'challenged' in some way, you must accomplish these tasks as a single unit remaining in direct and constant physical contact with each other. If you break contact in any way, you must return to your original starting position and 're-choose' body parts before attempting another crossing."

If you have a group of three, cut it down to three legs, two hands, two eyes, and one mouth. If you have to make a group of five add another leg (if you want).

The most challenging part of this activity has been keeping the groups accountable for following directions. The multiple unit groups make this hard to monitor. Younger groups are more challenging. The red flag for me has been if the unit groups are having a hard time following directions, then we tried this activity too soon. Something to consider.

This is a very challenging activity, but very interesting. Make every effort to emphasize being safe. Falling over during this activity is not uncommon if unit members are not helping each other. If the atmosphere becomes chaotic and/or unsafe, stop right away. Talk about how important all the members of the classroom are and why we should take care of each other. You might even choose to stop the activity for the day and wait for a better time to present it. In any case, I recommend that you save this one until your class has had time to do some lower-level problem-solving activities. I like to use CLASSROOM PARTS before a big unit project when the students will be working in groups this size. It's a good opportunity to practice the communication process between the group members.

OBSERVATION/QUESTIONS:

- Explain the process used to designate body parts.
- Was there a leader in this process?
- What sort of leadership style was used?
- Was everyone able to follow the guidelines of the activity?
- Did anyone have to compromise during the selection process?
- Did anyone choose not to compromise during the process?
- What might be good about compromising?
- What might be bad about compromising?
- What body part(s) were you?
- If there was an initial leader, was this leader the mouth? Why?
- How many people got to be the body part they wanted? How did you feel if you didn't get this part? In what way were your feelings expressed? Was this helpful to the unit process?
- What did your group do when finished? Help? Wait? Wait patiently? Encourage? Get into something else?
- How does this resemble other classroom activities?
- How would you grade your unit? How could you have gotten a better grade?
- What did you learn about this process that will help you in your upcoming project?
- What was the most challenging part of the activity for your unit? How did you meet the challenge?
- What was the most challenging part of the activity for each unit member? How did you meet the challenge?

(OTHERS)
-
-

VARIATIONS:

- For a little more challenge, do not allow a student to use two of the same body parts (e.g., two students will each have to use one eye).

OTHER IDEAS:

DON'T SPILL THE BEANS —

Joel Cryer via Tim Reed via Sam Sikes

NEEDS: One bandanna or a sheet of 8 1/2" x 11" paper and one good-size cup for every two or three players in the group. You will also need some stuff to put in the cups. I use beans. (After you're done with this activity, you can make soup.)

PROCEDURE: The over-all idea behind this one will be to move the beans from one place to another. Leave your room in the normal set-up and have the pairs (or groups of three) gather near any of the walls in your room. Hand out the supplies to each group and explain the guidelines:

1) Each small group must touch all four walls together.

2) Move as a group. Each player's hands must be touching the bandanna or paper at all times during movement.

3) The cup of beans must be on top of the bandanna or paper. If it falls, put the beans back in the cup and continue the process.

When groups finish, what do they do? What do you think would benefit the most?

OBSERVATIONS/QUESTIONS:

- What were some overall observations of the activity? What happened?
- What sort of communication went on before the beans started moving?
- How did groups communicate?
- What was the frustration level during the moving?
- What was the reaction to "spilling the beans"? How well did your group re-group?
- Did anyone come up with a plan to help move the beans?
- Did anyone have a plan they didn't share? Why?
- Did anyone ask for help?
- What worked well for you?..the group as a whole?
- What didn't work so well?
- If you were to do it again, what would make the process more productive?
-
-

(OTHERS)

125

VARIATIONS:

•The via Sam Sikes version. In small groups of three to eight, have them take hold of a bandanna by the edges so that everyone has both hands on it. Pull it taut and make it flat. "I will place a cup of water in the middle of the bandanna. You may not let go of the bandanna. The edges of the bandanna must always be below the top of the cup. Without spilling any water or letting go of the bandanna, follow me. Should you spill any water, we will start over." Move slowly so that the group can keep up with you. Make obstacles comparable to the group's ability. Finish the exercise by asking the team to place the bandanna and cup on the floor. This one is a good outdoor version.

OTHER IDEAS:

CHRIS-CROSS —

POSSIBLE OBJECTIVES: Trust, Problem Solving, Sharing, Cooperation, Helping...

NEEDS: One hula-hoop for every four players and one extra (small groups could be divided in threes). I usually borrow the hoops from the PE Department. You can also create shapes on the floor with masking tape. You will also need one 8 1/2" x 11" piece of paper for each player.

The set up is important. The hula-hoops or shapes are set up like a clock (see diagram - if you have twelve groups you are set! - but if you don't, you'll figure it out). Place the extra hoop in the middle, then set the other hoops five good-sized steps away from the center hoop with an equal distance between them around the circumference of the clock shape - that's one big step for each person in the small group, plus one extra step. (This is another good out-door activity if you can get there.) Adjust for smaller group size - keep in mind the action that will be taking place during the activity - group members will be stepping on their paper (you hope). If you are working on a slick floor, don't make the steps too far apart - the paper may slip out from under a long step. Now, if the group members tend to set them out too far, you will have to deal with the safety of this when it happens (because you're not going to tell them they cannot do this during the directions). Well, you might have to read this a few times. (If you're a visual person, get a bunch of people together, have a workshop, and we'll visit!)

Hoop Set-up

PROCEDURE: Gather together in teams of four for this one (be creative with left-overs - my mom always said). Give each player a sheet of paper and have them write their name on it - real big. With paper in hand, ask each "team" to position themselves by a hula-hoop or shape so you can give instructions.

My intention for this activity (but I don't tell them outright) is for players, in small groups, to start in one of the perimeter hoops, using their sheets of paper to step on as they travel to the center hoop. After stepping inside the center hoop, each player must find another hoop to stand in - excluding their original and center hoop - without touching the ground. If at any time someone touches the ground, that player must return to his/her original hoop to start again. To tell them all of this would be too easy for an adventure. So to add a bit of a twist I give each small group a copy of the following rhyme:

127

>   •   < < < < < < < < < < < < < < < < < < < < < < <

"All in your group will start inside a hoop.
To be fleet of feet, you must use your sheet.
Each must make a loop touching the space in the center hoop.
A new place you must find to end your journey, to unwind.
If any open ground you touch, return to your starting space.
Please take care in your travels, for surely this is not a race."

>   •   < < < < < < < < < < < < < < < < < < < < < < <

In this way the players become the experts. It's also interesting to watch what happens to this information during the activity.

NOTE: Younger groups may find it difficult to decipher the poem, so I usually just give them a straightforward set of directions. Still, don't tell them to leave their paper behind.

Presenting the introduction notice I used the words "team" and "group." What do you think will happen? Will the group work together or separate into teams? My hope with this activity is that each person will leave their paper (themselves) at the disposal of the group - leave it on the ground in a path to the center. All groups must have a "center," a place of reference. And it takes each member of that group to support that place (I'm rambling). You would be surprised at what happens to the paper, especially when someone has their name on it - interesting.

OBSERVATIONS/QUESTIONS:
- Describe the actions of your team during the activity.
- Describe some actions of the class during the activity.
- How were the papers handled? Were there possession issues?
- Evaluate the role of the player with the directions.
- What are the benefits of directions?
- How well were the directions followed?
- Describe some conflicting interpretations of the directions/SOPs.
- How were these conflicts resolved?
- What is the difference between a group and a team?
- As a class, do we sometimes split into teams? When? What are some benefits of doing this?
- What was the end result of the group activity?
-
-

(OTHERS)

128

VARIATIONS:

•Give out only one rhyme sheet for the entire class. (This is very interesting.)
•Give out one line of the rhyme to five different players in the class.

OTHER IDEAS:

POKER FACE ──

Donna & Kenny Allen

POSSIBLE OBJECTIVES: Accepting Diversity, Accepting Limitations, Non-Verbal Communication, Verbal Communication, Inclusion, Decision Making...

NEEDS: You will need a standard deck of playing cards, the bigger the better. You could also use alphabet cards if you have less than 27 kids in your class.

PROCEDURE: Clear the center of your room making a good-size play area. Hand each student a card. Tell them they are not to look at the face of the card now or at any point during the game. I like to have them hold the card so the character is facing down toward the floor as I explain the directions.

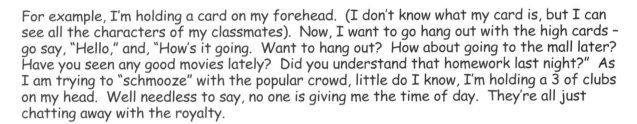

This activity involves the students mingling around the room, holding their card on their forehead, and treating each other by the value of the cards they are seeing. The king has the most value in this game and the ace has the least (when using the alphabet, "A" has the highest value). The trick is not to tell anyone what the character on his or her card is. So, the idea is to associate with the high character cards - tens and up - and stay away from the low level cards without actually telling other players what their cards are.

For example, I'm holding a card on my forehead. (I don't know what my card is, but I can see all the characters of my classmates). Now, I want to go hang out with the high cards – go say, "Hello," and, "How's it going. Want to hang out? How about going to the mall later? Have you seen any good movies lately? Did you understand that homework last night?" As I am trying to "schmooze" with the popular crowd, little do I know, I'm holding a 3 of clubs on my head. Well needless to say, no one is giving me the time of day. They're all just chatting away with the royalty.

Hope you get the idea here. Some groups may struggle with thinking of things to say. This "mingling" relation is great to observe (see Observations/Questions).

The fun doesn't end here. After sufficient mingling, ask the students to stop talking and stand still – DON'T LOOK AT THE CARDS YET! Tell the students to line up in a circle (It is possible. I would love to tell you about a conversation I had with some five-year-olds on this topic, but I'll save it for another time), in the order of the card value they think they are. (You might want to help them with a starting and ending point.) For this game, the value they line up in is based on how they were treated during the mingling. When everyone has a place in the circle, ask the students to look around the room at the order of cards on each player's forehead, then look at their own card. How did they do?

NOTE: This game can bring up some interesting emotions that you may have to deal with. These are the learning moments! Some learning moments are more powerful than others for different people. Keep a watchful eye over all your students. Make sure they leave the activity with their esteem intact. I like to do a round of BLUE CARDS after this one.

OBSERVATIONS/QUESTIONS:

- Who is moving about the room? Are they pro-active or de-active? Is this character consistent with the student?
- How did we do?
- How were you aware of your "position" in relation to others?
- How was the activity for you? What were some feelings that came up for you?
- On what basis were you judging and being judged?
- In what way is this like the world? Your community? Your school?
- What can we do to prevent judgement based on appearances?
- Did you seek out the high cards? Did others seek you out? How did this make you feel?
- Were you ever overwhelmed during the activity? In what way?
- Did anyone just want to quit and look at their card? Why?
- What was it like to get a lot of attention? Is this normal for you?
- If you had the choice, would you like more or less attention from others?
- What was it like not getting any attention? Is this normal for you?
- What do you feel like when people don't give you attention?
- What are some good/bad ways we get attention from others?
- How much attention do you need from friends? Peers? Teachers? Parents? Adults?
- Did this activity teach you anything?
- (OTHERS)
-
-

VARIATIONS:

- For a very interesting process I like to stack the deck a bit. I'll put three or four low cards at the bottom of the deck. Then, by slight of hand, I'll pull bottom cards out for some of the more popular students so they can experience how others will treat them.

OTHER IDEAS:

131

PEER PRESSURE —

Donna & Kenny Allen

POSSIBLE OBJECTIVES: Open discussion about Peer Pressure, Decision Making, Verbal Communication, Trust...

NEEDS: No special props are needed for this one.

PROCEDURE: This activity is a wonderful catalyst for a discussion on peer pressure. The process does digress a bit from the format of this book because only a few people will really get to experience the situation, but we felt the processing potential of PEER PRESSURE was well worth sharing.

Ask for four volunteers (I like to choose two girls and two boys) who are willing to sit in front of the class.

> Note: These volunteers will be subject to verbal suggestions by their classmates to get out of the chairs. I never allow any physical touching of any kind or swearing, but, the more creative taunters may come up with some verbal suggestions that could elicit emotional responses from the volunteers. I would suggest that you choose students that have some emotional stability, that can accept what is happening, and can share the experience with the class. Just wanted to put the thought in your head. The bottom line is that we try to keep our activities physically and emotionally safe. Our kids might experience some physical and emotional tension, but we should always bring them back to their comfort zone before all is said and done.

Take the volunteers "out of eye-shot" of the rest of the class so you can give them some "secret" instructions (the hallway is usually a good spot). Tell these brave souls that they will be sitting in chairs at the front of the class. Tell them that no matter what happens they are not to get out of their chairs (unless there is a school drill of some sort) until you give them instructions to do so. Assure them that no physical harm will come to them. Ask these volunteers to stay in the hallway while you go into the room and give the other students their "secret" instructions.

Tell the remainder of the class that their goal is to get the volunteers out of their chairs. At no time can the volunteers, or their chairs, be touched in any way by anything (this goes for spitting - we had to add this rule after a very emotional incident but, I must add, a very powerful and positive one in the end). There will also be no swearing of any kind (you will probably have to define this). I assign small groups to each volunteer, and challenge them to get their volunteer out of the chair for a special prize. There will be a first, second and

132

third prize – the volunteer can share in the special prize as well. (Is this pressure? What is it when adults give children "verbal suggestions" to meet an end – not peer pressure? Just a ponder point for you.)

At this point, I ask if anyone has any questions. When all is clear, we ask the volunteers back into the room and set them up in front. Leave enough space around each volunteer for the verbal suggesters to have access to them. Then, let the games begin.

Be sure to monitor as much of the action as possible. Stop anything that is inappropriate. Continue the activity until you feel the actions warrant enough discussion. We like to have enough situations to draw from.

About the special prize – you really don't have one. In this case your pressure had no benefit. (Get ready to talk about this!)

OBSERVATIONS/QUESTIONS:
•Who volunteered? Why? Who didn't you choose? Why?
•What were the secret instructions for the volunteers?
•What was it like sitting in the chairs? Easy? Difficult?
•Did you ever want to get out of the chair? When?
•Did you get out of the chair? Why?
•Who gave the volunteers their secret instructions? What motivated them to follow the instructions? If the volunteers had been offered a special prize, would it have been easier for them to follow the instructions? Why?
•What were the secret instructions for the rest of the class?
•Did the rest of the class have any incentive to follow their instructions? How was the incentive useful?
•How did you feel when you found out there really was no special prize? Has this situation ever happened to you before? What does this do to your trust level?
•Did you use positive or negative verbal suggestions to move your volunteer?
•In what way is this activity related to our classroom or school community?
•What is peer pressure? Is it good or bad? Can it be both? How?
•How does peer pressure relate to trust?
•Let's check in with everyone. How are we feeling at this point? What can we learn from this activity?
•
•

(OTHERS)

VARIATIONS:

133

OTHER IDEAS:
•You might want to play BLUE CARDS after this one to bring the energy back up.

WIRED —

POSSIBLE OBJECTIVES: Trust, Listening, Helping, Decision Making...

NEEDS: Provide two paper clips for each pair of students. I like to start out with the big paper clips and have the smaller ones available for an added challenge. (There are giant paper clips that work great. Any office supply store carries them.)

PROCEDURE: First we will need to establish some terminology. Look at a paper clip. There are three bends in a regular clip - two bends near one end and one bend at the other. Look at the end with the two bends. There is an outside bend and an inside bend. (The inside bend is the one "inside" the clip. Imagine a paper clip without an inside bend. Would it be able to clip? Sorry, I get sidetracked easily.) The inside bend is the key to setting up.

Take two paper clips and attach them together so the two "inside" bends are interlocked. If you were to pull the clips apart using the single bend ends, only the inside bends would be touching (an initiative in itself). Do you have it? (If you can think of an easier way to explain it on paper, please let us know.) Make enough of these wire puzzles for your group. (Or, have each set of partners put them together, each holding their own paper clip in one hand – another activity that might unlock some doors!?)

Now for the game. Partner up students and have one of them pick up the interlocking clips. Ask the player holding the clips to close their eyes. Now have the other partner, who is sighted, verbally instruct the unsighted partner in the steps to take apart the clips. The unsighted partners can only do what the sighted partners are telling them. How many students just work ahead of the directions? The sighted partners cannot touch any part of the clips or their partner during the game. Also, the clips may not be bent out of their original shape during the game (this is an optional rule).

After all the clips are apart, switch roles and try again.

> NOTE: I've done this activity two different ways. Do not give the pairs any time to plan, just jump into it and experience the process the first round, each player trying the clips without problem-solving in between. After both have had their turn, have the pair discuss and problem-solve, then they each can try again. The other way I've done it was to discuss and problem-solve after the first player has taken the clips apart and before the second player starts. It will depend on the time you have for the activity. The first suggestion takes a bit longer.

The biggest hitch to be aware of is timing. Some pairs finish much earlier than others.
Let the pairs talk quietly about their experience or observe others to fill the time.

OBSERVATIONS/QUESTIONS:
•Was this activity easy or difficult?
•What made it easy or difficult?
•Did anyone get frustrated? What was frustrating?
•Did anyone give up on their partner? Why?
•Did anyone work ahead of the directions? Is this good or bad?
•Did any of the unsighted players peek? Why?
•How did you feel when you got the clips apart?
•Who had the more important role during the game?
•Were you able to communicate well with your partner?
•What does good communication involve?
•What did you learn from this activity that might help you in the classroom?
(OTHERS)
•
•

VARIATIONS:
•Try this activity without using words. Kids are great at mouth noises.
•I've seen this idea used more than once. Before the WIRED activity, give each stu-
 dent a paper clip, and ask them how many uses they can think of for a paper clip.
 The idea promotes creative exploration. Looking at things in a different way.
 Looking outside of the box, etc.
•Have students put a small boxed puzzle together.

OTHER IDEAS:

DRIVING IN THE DARK—

POSSIBLE OBJECTIVES: Trust, Non-Verbal Communication, Trust, Decision Making... (Did I mention that there could be some trust development here?!)

NEEDS: If you want to provide a choice for students, bring in some blindfolds for half of your class. Don't forget, any time you use blindfolds, please make them optional. Students can also just close their eyes. That way if there is a need to see, the student can choose to open his eyes. Students are also allowed to take off their blindfold at any time.

PROCEDURE: Arrange your room with the desks in rows – between the rows will be streets. If you have the space, try to provide some room between the desks in the rows for alleys. Also, create enough room around the outside area of the desks to have a two-lane highway (a nice oval track so to speak).

Ask the students to get into pairs with someone they would be willing to work with. The key word here is "willing." There might be some students that will need to compromise. (You will also want to do this activity when you have an even number of students in your class. You won't be able to play because you will need to watch for safety issues.) Ask each pair to stand somewhere out on the highway (never the real one) and choose who will be the first car and who will be the first driver. The first car dons the blindfold or closes their eyes. The driver stands behind the car and uses the following non-verbal cues to direct their partner, the car:

1. No contact - the car moves forward.
2. Both hands on the shoulders - stop.
3. Hand on the left shoulder - turn left.
4. Hand on the right shoulder - turn right.
5. Pointer finger touching the cars back - reverse.
(You could write these directions on the board as a reference if you think there is a need.)

Before anyone starts their engine (and maybe even before the blindfolds are in place), have some discussion about trust. What are some issues the students might have with trust? With their partner? What are some things you and your partner can do to prove that you are trustworthy? When there seems to be a good idea about the expectations, have the cars (with the lights out) put up their bumpers (all cars have bumpers, right?) The bumpers-up position is elbows comfortably at the sides, forearms up parallel to the ground (90 degree angle in the elbows), and hands open with fingers extended toward the sky (another 90 degree angle in the wrists). This will provide a little up-front protection - but watch out for those desks. They can cause an awesome "charley horse" in the leg.

Start your engines! (Sound effects are cool here.) Call out "Highway driving." This is the cue for the drivers to move their cars around the highway area (around the outside of the desks) using the non-verbal actions described above. Keep a very watchful eye out for traffic violations, and stop the action immediately if something unsafe occurs. When all the car and driver teams seem to have the hang of it, call "Pit stop." This is the signal to stop and switch places. The driver will become the car and the car the driver. "Start your engines. Highway driving." When the new driver has the hang of things, call "Pit stop" again. "Start your engines. City driving." As I bet you have guessed, city driving is down and around the desks. Drivers are still allowed to use the highway, but they may not travel more than halfway around the room before entering back into the city streets. "Pit stop." Switch out car and driver. "City driving." "Pit stop." Now we should be back with the original car and driver.

You might want to take a little break from the action at this point to discuss any issues that might have occurred before you move into the second leg of the rally.

The second leg is not much different than the first. However, this time you will not be so structured. All the non-verbal cues are the same, all the verbal directions are the same. But this time you can use the verbal directions in any order at any time. Let's review:

> "Start your engines" - give a little preparation before movement.
> "Highway driving" - moving the cars around the outside of the desks.
> "City driving" - moving the cars among the desks.
> "Pit stop" - first stop, then change car and driver positions.

Let the pairs know that you are always talking to the driver when you give your verbal directions. Here's a little sample: "Start your engines. Highway driving. City driving. Pit stop. City driving. Highway driving. Pit stop. Girls, city driving. Boys, city driving. Girls, highway driving. Boys, pit stop." So, I think you have the idea. Make sure you stop while it's still fun. They will be more willing to play again another time.

> NOTE: When all is said and done, safety is most important. Always stop the activity (and this goes for any activity) if anyone is being unsafe. If the trust level goes down with some students in your group, you will have to work that much harder with your whole group to bring the trust level back up.

Have fun out there and remember "always hang up before you drive."

OBSERVATIONS/QUESTIONS:
•Did anyone have any apprehensions before starting?
•What happened during the test driving leg?
•What was your partner doing that was helpful?
•What suggestions might you give your partner to improve his driving skills?
•What was hard about this sort of communication? When is this sort of communication good?..bad? (Watch out here, this could open up some deep issues)
•Does anyone wish to change partners?
•What was the difference between highway and city driving?
•How did your bumpers help you?
•What sorts of bumpers do we have? What do they protect us from?
•Did anyone choose to open their eyes? Why?
•What quality or qualities did you and your partner have to share to be successful?
•How do we build trust with each other? What breaks down trust?
•What is important about trusting someone?

•What did you or your partner do to prove that you were trustworthy?
•What are some thoughts about the trust level in this class?
•What are some thoughts about the trust level in this school?
•Who's ready for their driver's license?
(OTHERS)
•
•

VARIATIONS:

•You could move to the third leg of the rally – sponge tag. Get a few dry, soft sponges and toss them into the city. Start the cars and drivers out on the highway. Drivers want to direct their car to a sponge, have their car pick the sponge up and throw it at another car – the driver gives the coordinates. If a car hits another car or driver with a sponge, they earn a point for their tandem. Call a "pit stop" every now and then to change cars and drivers. Which tandem can score the most points in the allotted time?

OTHER IDEAS:

BOOK RETURN —

Kip Prichard via Sam Sikes

POSSIBLE OBJECTIVES: Trust, Problem Solving, Listening, Verbal Communication, Decision Making, Helping...

NEEDS: Each student will need a book (a small one works the best) with their name inside. It's more challenging to use the same book for each student or no more than three different kinds of books - possibly a workbook or small novel they might be reading for a unit assignment. You could use a text book, but you must be extra careful not to drop it on toes. You will also need some masking tape and something to mark boundaries – desks might work depending on the room you have. Bring in some blindfolds for half the class if you are comfortable with using them with your students.

PROCEDURE: You will want to clear the center of the room and make as much open space as possible. With the masking tape, create a square in the center of the room big enough to hold all the books - books can be stacked two high. If the desks work as an outside boundary, use them as the edge of the "learning zone." Students can be touching the desks as they work. You could also lay out boundaries in any other creative way that works for your room.

Here's how the game works. Students will be working in pairs - you can choose the pairs or leave it up to the students. A group of three will also work. The age of the students may determine what you will do. The objective will be for all the students to obtain their own book in as little time as possible. (Please read that again - especially the "ALL" part. You don't have to give it away. At least not yet.)

What's the catch? Any student in the learning zone - the space between the books and the outside (desk) boundaries - must have their eyes closed - or be blindfolded. The blinded players will be guided by their sighted partners who will be standing outside the learning zone. When a blinded player obtains a book, he brings it back to the sighted partner. (Remember, the blinded player still needs guidance, as he must remain blinded while in the learning zone.) Once the blinded player reaches his partner, he opens his eyes (removes blindfold) and checks to see if the book belongs to the sighted partner. If it does, set it down outside the learning zone. Now the sighted partner will be the next blinded retriever, and the blinded partner will be the sighted guide (they switched roles). If the book does not belong to the first sighted partner, it must be returned by the newly blinded player who then brings back another book. (Here's the little catch. Make sure you just say "returned." But returned to where?)

Let's see if I can sum this up. Only sighted guides outside of the learning zone can accept their own book. Only blinded players can retrieve one book at a time. When both players have their book...then what? "To be or not to be helpful" is the question - don't tell them. See what happens.

140

This activity, as you have already guessed, takes a great deal of trust. Taking away someone's eyesight is a great challenge. Please make sure you do this activity when the group has built some trust through other classroom activities. If you see any unsafe actions, stop right away. Correct the problem and move on, or correct the problem and change activities. You can come back to this one later. If you don't use the blindfolds and ask the students to close their eyes, they have the opportunity to open them if they feel the need to do so. If there are a number of eye openers, this should be an eye opener. There is a low level of trust with some people. Stop the activity and find out what can be done to raise the trust level so you can continue the activity following the fulfillment of those requirements. So much to learn in so little time. Whatever you do, keep it fun!

Once the students complete this first stage you will have a "time to beat." (You did time it, right?) Some groups may not get the helpful return part, so go into some processing questions. When you get to the "did anyone return it to the owner" question, the lights may go on. The group might want to try the activity again, for a better time, using the cooperative strategies some of them will be brainstorming. Of course it will be up to the time you have. You can always come back to the cooperative method another day.

OBSERVATIONS/QUESTIONS:
- What did you observe during this activity?
- Can you share some of the important skills we had to have for this activity?
- Share some qualities the small teams had to have?
- Did you trust your partner?
- What were some things your partner did to gain your trust?
- Was there anything your partner did to take away some of your trust?
- When you lose trust in someone, what does it take to gain that trust back? Is it easy?
- What are some things we can do to build trust in our class?
- What did you do when you and your partner had your books?
- What were some things you did to be helpful?
- What did you do with a book that wasn't yours?
- Did anyone "return" the book to its owner? Why not?
- How would this have affected the time of the activity?
- Do all of us finish our work at the same time? What does this do for our class?
- How much more could we do if we were more helpful to one another?
- What would you like to do if we had extra time in class?
-
-

(OTHERS)

141

VARIATIONS:

·Instead of books, you could use 3" x 5" note cards. Have each student write something on the card that they like to do. Have them obtain a card. Will players find other cards with things they like to do?

·You can also put each student's name on a 3" x 5" card and have them find themselves - wouldn't that be nice?

OTHER IDEAS:

CHALLENGE FIELD ━━

Karl Rohnke

POSSIBLE OBJECTIVES: Trust, Listening, Trust, Verbal Communication, Trust, Helping, Trust, Patience...

NEEDS: A lot of small objects from around your room for obstacles, blindfolds for half the group and a medium-size open area to play. Masking tape for a boundary is helpful but not necessary.

PROCEDURE: Create a "challenge field" within a large open space in the center of your room with the various objects (the more the better). Arrange all the small objects around the floor so that they are randomly and equally spaced.

Pair up students in any way you choose. Give each pair a blindfold (remember, there is always the choice to use the blindfold or to close your eyes). The objective will be for one partner to cross the challenge field blindfolded without touching any of the objects (you can see, the more objects, the better). The sighted partner, who is standing outside the challenge field, is not allowed to touch the blindfolded partner on the field or to go onto the field during the activity. They can only verbally guide their partners across. Provide time for each person to try the activity a couple of times.

If possible, work in groups of three with one member timing the pass through the challenge field. For each object the blind trekker touches, add 30 seconds to their time. If timing is not possible, count the number of touches for a player and try to lower it the second time they cross. Even better, add the number of touches both partners obtain together and try to do better a second time as a team.

If you can make a large challenge field, all the pairs can go at once. This causes some communication difficulty and adds to processability. When students are done, have them try some of the variations.

OBSERVATIONS/QUESTIONS:
- What was difficult about the activity?
- How did partners communicate? Did it work?
- What did you learn about communication?
- How did each person feel when the blinded partner touched an object?
- Was the trust level affected after a touch?
- How did sighted partners respond when their partners touched an object?
- What feelings came up during the activity?
- Was there any goal setting done before the activity?
- What was it like to achieve or not achieve your goal?
-
-

(OTHERS)

VARIATIONS
·Blindfolded partner walks backward.
·Every command means the opposite - right means left, big step means small step, bend down means stand up. You get the idea.
·Work in groups of threes. One person guides two connected players.

OTHER IDEAS:

EXPERIENTIAL LUNCH—

POSSIBLE OBJECTIVES: Trust, Problem Solving, Listening, Verbal Communication, Decision Making, Helping, Patience, Sharing, Listening, Responsibility...

NEEDS: You will need blindfolds for half of your class - bandannas work well. This activity is somewhat elaborate but well worth the effort. You and your class will be planning a picnic – in class or not (outside always lends itself to added adventure). EXPERIENTIAL LUNCH does consume a good deal of time. I would also suggest that the activity be held in a place that is easy to clean up.

So, the needs will be lunch stuff. You know - plates, napkins, forks, sandwich stuff, chips, potato salad, and drinks - stay away from the darker drinks (just trust me).

PROCEDURE: Make plans with your class to have lunch. If you have parents that are willing to get involved, get them aboard. You can go as far as making a list of needed items and assigning students to bring something in (remember I told you this would be a little work). The more items you can "put together" during your lunch the better, e.g., peanut butter and jelly sandwiches, coldcuts-cheese-lettuce sandwiches with catsup and mustard, etc. So far this is an initiative in itself, but a great learning experience.

Here's how it works. On the big day set up all the items on a long table. Don't put anything together, just open everything and set it out. When everyone is ready for lunch (hands washed, etc.), pair up classmates. (This probably wouldn't be the best time to pair up students that don't get along.)

Tell students that this will be an exercise in communication and following directions. Before you start, each pair must decide between them who will be the Instruction Specialist (IS) and who will be the Construction Specialist (CS) - who would be willing to be blindfolded. When the choices are made, place the blindfold on the CS and ask the IS to place her hands behind her back - she will not be allowed to use her hands until the CS removes his blindfold.

With everyone in the "good to go" position, explain to the students that they will be working together with their partners to: 1) make their lunches; 2) sit down and eat their lunches; and 3) with their physical challenges removed, clean up together - hopefully in that order. Sometimes the clean up part moves its way up in the order!? After the moans and groans, give a few more instructions. Ask the ISs to be very specific in giving directions. The CSs should follow the directions to the letter. This means that they are to do only what the IS tells them to do and no more.

THE BOTTOM LINE: One partner (CS) cannot see, and the other (IS) may not use her hands. The IS verbally guides the lunch-making process for both - so, maybe make one lunch at a time. The CS will be doing the feeding for both of them. The IS will be giving the directions for both of them. Again, during the cleaning process both partners are back to full use of all their capable faculties.

Overall it is a very powerful exercise in trust, not to mention all the other things that happen. Be sure all the students know that they may discard their physical challenges at any time. Encourage them to hang in there, but always give them the option. I have only used this activity with groups who are really willing to dive into this adventure. It has always been a great hit.

OBSERVATIONS/QUESTIONS:
·What part did the students take in the planning process? Who was involved? Who wasn't?
·What did you like about the planning process?
·Was there any leadership in this process? Was this leader accepted by everyone?
·Did everyone bring something to the lunch? Why is this important?
·What was the reaction to the task?
·How many pairs were able to get through to the cleaning process?
·Who decided to challenge out? Could you share some reasons for doing so?
·What was the experience like for the Instruction Specialists (giving directions, not being able to help, being fed by someone)?
·What was it like for the Construction Specialists (not being able to see, feeding someone)?
·What was the most challenging aspect of the activity?
·What was the most powerful feeling you experienced during the activity?
·What do you think might be important about helping each other?
·In what ways can we help each other more in the classroom?
(OTHERS) ·
·

VARIATIONS:
·Do the activity without a blindfold. The key here is that the CS must do exactly what they are told. (The older kids seem to catch this one a bit better.)
Try this activity with any related task, such as gift wrapping a box, putting to-gether a small puzzle, or building an object with blocks or other construction materials available to you.
·Have each of the partners (both sighted) put one hand behind their back and create their lunch by sharing the task using only one hand each. To make this even more challenging, ask them to put their dominant hand behind them.

OTHER IDEAS:

THE SHOES—
Experiential Community

POSSIBLE OBJECTIVES: Sharing, Inclusion, Decision Making, Patience, Accepting Feedback, Non-Verbal Communication...

NEEDS: If all of your students wear shoes to school, you're set for this one. Oh, and you need just a little masking tape.

PROCEDURE: I really make an effort not to qualify my activities based on the age group they are most appropriate for, because I have been proven wrong in almost every case. However, THE SHOES is one that still can be qualified in my book. This is a very esoterically metaphorical activity (the biggest words you'll ever read from me). So, the spirit of THE SHOES tends to be most successful with older kids, 8th grade and older. Why did I put this one in if it has limited use? It's a very powerful way to get students to talk to each other. Some of my most memorable experiences have taken place around THE SHOES.

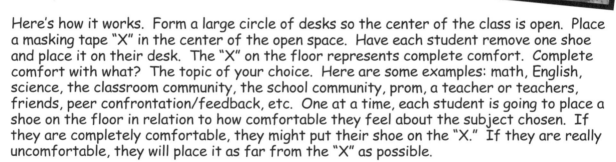

Here's how it works. Form a large circle of desks so the center of the class is open. Place a masking tape "X" in the center of the open space. Have each student remove one shoe and place it on their desk. The "X" on the floor represents complete comfort. Complete comfort with what? The topic of your choice. Here are some examples: math, English, science, the classroom community, the school community, prom, a teacher or teachers, friends, peer confrontation/feedback, etc. One at a time, each student is going to place a shoe on the floor in relation to how comfortable they feel about the subject chosen. If they are completely comfortable, they might put their shoe on the "X." If they are really uncomfortable, they will place it as far from the "X" as possible.

After every student has placed their shoe on the floor, observe the placements. You could spend a little processing time here.

OBSERVATIONS/QUESTIONS:
- Where is your shoe?
- Why did you place your shoe where it is?
- What are some reasons you have for being comfortable?
- What are you uncomfortable about?
- What could be done to achieve a higher level of comfort for you?
- Is there something you could ask or share with the class that might increase your comfort level on the subject?

(OTHERS)
-
-

After some dialog with the students, allow additional time for the students to change the placement of their shoe if they feel the need. They can change it more than once. You could ask, "Is there a place in the circle that would make you more comfortable about the subject?" This is where the deep part fits in. Do the students move their shoes near another shoe? Do they place shoes on top of each other? Do they change the direction of the shoe? Is the shoe upside down?

There are some very interesting issues that tend to surface, things that you might not be aware of. The students I have worked with like to "talk to the shoes." They can throw their concerns out into the room. THE SHOES also allows the opportunity to give feedback and support to one another. If you leave the atmosphere open and allow the needed time to talk, things will happen. When you have the sense that your kids need to talk - start by talking to THE SHOES.

MORE OBSERVATIONS/QUESTIONS:
  •Where did you move your shoe?
  •Why did you move the shoe there?
  •What is the significance of the direction of your shoe?
  •How are our shoes the same? How are they different?
  •Who is sharing? How do you feel about speaking in front of the class?
  •What would it take for you to feel completely comfortable?
  •What subject are you completely comfortable with?
(OTHERS) •
  •

VARIATIONS:
  •Instead of shoes, place yourself somewhere on the floor.

OTHER IDEAS:

THE CAR WASH—
Jack Canfield

POSSIBLE OBJECTIVES: Sharing, Accepting Feedback, Support...

NEEDS: Nothing extra needed.

PROCEDURE: This activity consists simply of lining up your class in two parallel lines fairly close together. Then one student is sent through the wash (between the lines) and everyone touches him or her (being appropriate is important here) and says words of praise and affection and encouragement. The pats on the back, handshaking, and verbal support produce a sparkling, shiny, happy "car" at the end of the wash!

We usually run one or two people through the car wash each day rather than everybody in one big cleanup. This insures that the responses of the washers are fresh, personalized and enthusiastic. However, putting everyone through the car wash at the end of an intensive experience is a great way to end a session.

OBSERVATIONS/QUESTIONS:
We don't tend to process this one at all; we just let it happen.

VARIATIONS:
·Put the two lines near the door and car wash a few people before they go home.

OTHER IDEAS:
·Don't forget to get a wash yourself every once in a while.

From Jack Canfield, 100 Ways to Enhance Self-Concept in the Classroom, © 1976 by Allyn & Bacon. Adapted by permission.

CREATING THE ENVIRONMENT:
A COMMUNITY BUILDING SEQUENCE

A sense of community does not just automatically occur. The conditions must be right. Witness the breakdown in community in some neighborhoods, while others continue to enjoy feelings of connection, sharing and support. There are some classrooms where students feel safe to make mistakes, are given encouragement from their peers, and have the opportunity to take responsibility for their learning. In other classrooms, students are lucky to know the names of a few people by the end of the semester.

Creating a sense of community begins when the teacher chooses to focus on it. Most teachers already have structures in place that allow for the seeds of community to be sewn. The following chart will help you plan a sequence of activities that can help these seeds bear fruit.

In this sequence each level builds upon the other, with skills and issues developed to support the growing level of trust and interaction between students. Each stage takes into account the developmental level of the group, issues that must be addressed before heading to the next level, and activities that can be used to help students gain necessary experience and discuss issues.

In designing a plan for each class, the issues at each level must be addressed. For example, in the cooperation level, if students continue to call each other names (put-downs), or refuse to work with some of the people (mixing), it will be impossible to build trust. During the trust level, if students laugh at each other when a mistake is made (making mistakes) or try to hurt each other during trust activities (lack of empathy), they will be unable to solve problems together as equals.

When introducing the sequence to the class, build ownership by showing the sequence to them. Begin creating a shared vision by telling them how the process works. Have goals, both large and small to work toward, and celebrate when goals are obtained. Focus on skills and issues that need focus, and acknowledge when the students have made a step forward. Ask them what they think about their progress. Become partners in the process.

Every class will work at its own pace. Some will get stuck at a level, while others fly through it. Later, the tables may turn. The job of the teacher is to assess the needs of the class and try to choose activities that help the class focus on issues that need to be addressed. The activities themselves do not push the group forward, they are only vehicles in which to help the process along. It is what we do with the activities that causes movement and gives us the opportunity to experience growth.

We put the activities in GAMES (& other stuff) FOR TEACHERS in this handy reference chart so that you can better plan your activity sequence. This Community Building Sequence is thoroughly described in "A Journey Into the Land of Heart," by Laurie Frank. Many activities will fit within different parts of the sequence depending on how they are presented. With a wide variety of options for you, this type of community building can

----------APPENDIX A--

151

bring a sense of adventure and fun to the learning process. An appropriate sequence provides the opportunity to create a robust sense of community to your classroom. In this safe and comfortable environment, students are able to look past their perceived limitations and take the necessary risks to learn from their mistakes, share new ideas, and solve conflicts peacefully.

COMMUNITY BUILDING SEQUENCE—

ACTIVITY	COOPERATION	TRUST	PROBLEM SOLVING
Are You More Like…	X	X	
Now & Later	X	X	
Quality Assurance	X		
The Big Question/30 Seconds	X	X	
You Tear Me Up	X		
Classroom Assumptions	X	X	
Chosen	X	X	
Letter Opener	X		X
Assumption Test		X	X
The Number Game			X
Group Number Game		X	X
P.S.	X	X	X
Simply Paper	X	X	X
Empathy	X		
Blue Cards	X	X	
Pencil, Paper & Popsicle Stick		X	X
Particulars			X
Roomination	X		X
Enumeration	X	X	X
Classroom Poetry	X		X
It's All in the Cards	X		X
Circle-a-Loons	X		
Balloon Bash	X		X
Objectables			X
Over the Top			X
A What?	X		
Quick Numbers	X	X	
Touch	X	X	X
Sensory Masterpiece	X		
The Mixing Game	X	X	
Front-to-Front	X	X	X
Cliques	X		X
Communication Box			X

GAMES (& other stuff) FOR TEACHERS, © 1999 CHRIS CAVERT/WOOD 'N' BARNES PUBLISHING & DISTRIBUTION

COMMUNITY BUILDING SEQUENCE (CON'T.) —

ACTIVITY	COOPERATION	TRUST	PROBLEM SOLVING
Gotcha Lines	X		
Centerpiece			X
A Very Large Knot			X
Toe Jam		X	X
Classroom Parts		X	X
Don't Spill the Beans			X
Chris-Cross			X
Poker Face	X		X
Peer Pressure		X	
Wired		X	X
Driving in the Dark	X	X	
Book Return	X	X	X
Challenge Field	X	X	
Experiential Lunch	X	X	X
The Shoes		X	
The Car Wash		X	

REFERENCES/RESOURCES

Aycox, F., (1985). Games we should play in school. Discovery Bay, CA: Front Row Experience. (800) 516-8919

Cain, J. & Jolliff, B., (1998). Teamwork & Teamplay. Dubuque, IA: Kendall/Hunt Publishing (800) 772-9165

Dobkin, Craig. You can contact Craig at: craigdobkin@playforpeace.org

Eckert, L., (1998). If anybody asks me...1001 questions for educators, counselors, and therapists. Oklahoma City, OK: Wood 'N' Barnes Publishing. (800) 678-0621

Frank, L., (2000). A journey into the land of heart: Creating community in the classroom and beyond. Hamilton, MA: Project Adventure.

Gerstein, J., (1994). Place of connection: Expressive counseling techniques for families and individuals. Oklahoma City, OK: Wood 'N' Barnes Publishing. (800) 678-0621

Highlights® for children, A monthly magazine for children 2 - 12. 1992. To contact the magazine, please call 717-253-1080, e-mail Highlights@ezaccess.net.

Knapp, C. E. (1988). Creating humane climates outdoors: A people skill primer. Charleston, WV: Appalachia Educational Laboratory.

Newstrom, J. W. & Scannell, E. E., (1980). Games trainers play. New York: McGraw Hill.

Rohnke, Karl (Karl has a number of books you can order through Kendall/Hunt. I highly recommend Quicksilver and the three volumes of FUNN Stuff). Call KH for their free "Hands on Learning: A Teachers Resource Catalog." (800) 772-9165

Sikes, S., (1998). Executive marbles: And other team building activities. Tulsa, OK: Learning Unlimited. (888) 622-4203

Trent, Scott. For more information about Scott's Building Block system, contact him at (888) 572-2725, or visit his web site: obbsystems.com

ADDITIONAL EXPERIENTIAL REFERENCES

Cavert, C., (1999). Affordable portables: A working-book of initiative activities & problem solving elements, Revised & expanded version. Oklahoma City, OK: Wood 'N' Barnes Publishing.

DeBolt, G. P., ed., (1996). Into the classroom: The Outward Bound approach to teaching and learning. Dubuque, IA: Kendall/Hunt Publishing

Henton, M., (1996). Adventure in the classroom: Using adventure to strengthen learning and build a community of life-long learners. Dubuque, IA: Kendall/Hunt Publishing

Horwood, B., (1995). Experience and the curriculum. Dubuque, IA: Kendall/Hunt Publishing

Knapp, C., (1992). Lasting lessons: A teacher's guide to reflecting on experience. Charleston, WV: Appalachia Educational Laboratory.

Nadler, R. S., & Luckner, J. L., (1997). Processing the experience: Strategies to enhance and generalize learning. Dubuque, IA: Kendall/Hunt Publishing

Schoel, J., Prouty, D., & Radcliffe, P., (1988). Islands of healing: A guide to adventure-based counseling. Hamilton, MA: Project Adventure.

Warren, K., Sakofs, M., & Hunt, J. S. ed., (1995). The theory of experiential education. Dubuque, IA: Kendall/Hunt Publishing

ABOUT THE AUTHORS __

CHRIS CAVERT has been a teacher for over 20 years. He has worked with youth and adult groups of all ages. Chris holds a Physical Education teaching degree from the University of Wisconsin-LaCrosse, and nears completion of a Masters degree in Experiential Education from Mankato State University. Some of his first writing was published in the best selling *Chicken Soup for the Soul* series by Jack Canfield and Mark Victor Hansen, and his activities have been published in books by Karl Rohnke, Jim Cain and Berry Jolliff. Since then Chris has written E.A.G.E.R. Curriculum; Games (& other stuff) for Group, Books 1 & 2; Affordable Portables: A Workbook of Activities and Problem Solving Elements; and 50 Ways to Use Your Noodle: Loads of Land Games with Foam Noodle Toys (coauthored with Sam Sikes).

LAURIE FRANK is a public school teacher who has worked in the adventure field for over 17 years. She began her career as a special education teacher in emotional disabilities, working with students of all ages. Her path diverged upon the discovery of adventure education and experiential methodologies. The need to develop community within the school setting was apparent, and the adventure philosophy seemed the perfect vehicle to achieve that goal.

Laurie was a leader in designing the nationally recognized Stress/Challenge Adventure Program for Madison (Wisconsin) Metropolitan School District, and wrote their curriculum, "Adventure in the Classroom," in 1988.

Currently, Laurie is the director of GOAL Consulting, working with school districts and nonprofit organizations around the country to develop adventure education programs for children and young adults. She wrote the Camp Manito-wish (Collaborative) Leadership Manual in 1997. She is currently collaborating on a book with Ambrose Panico entitled "Experiential Education for the Classroom Community," and her book, "A Journey Into the Land of Heart: Creating Community in the Classroom and Beyond," is due out during the 1999-2000 school year.

Laurie has been a Certified Trainer with Project Adventure since 1990. She is also the coordinator for the Central America initiative in Play for Peace, an organization that focuses on bringing children of conflicting cultures together through play. She received the Michael Stratton Practitioner of the Year award from the Association for Experiential Education in 1997.

WORKSHOP INFORMATION —

Chris and Laurie believe that educating our young people is becoming more and more of a challenge. But they work with children because it is in their hearts to do so – something you as educators can appreciate and identify with. They are constantly discovering and creating valuable activities and ideas that can easily add fun and magic to an educational setting.

Rich in content and activities, their workshops are a great way to encourage excitement and interest among other teachers, counselors, etc. in the experiential, pro-social learning that Chris and Laurie promote. Invite them for a conference. They would be more than happy to visit and play with you.

For workshop information contact:

Mony Cunningham
Wood 'N' Barnes Publishing & Distribution
800-678-0621

OH, JUST ONE MORE THING,

PLEASE, DON'T FORGET TO HAVE FUN!
THAT'S WHAT IT'S ALL ABOUT!